Scottish

50
Shared
texts

Photocopiable texts
for shared reading

Fiction, non-fiction,
poetry and drama

Annotated versions

Discussion prompts

**Gillian Turner &
Sylvia Clements**

Credits

Authors
Gillian Turner and
Sylvia Clements

Series Consultants
Fiona Collins and
Alison Kelly

Editor
Dulcie Booth

**Assistant
Editor**
Roanne Charles

Illustrations
David Peet/
Smallworld
Designs

**Series
Designer**
Anna Oliwa

Designer
Anna Oliwa

Text © 2003 Gillian Turner and Sylvia Clements
© 2003 Scholastic Ltd

Designed using Adobe InDesign

Published by Scholastic Ltd
Villiers House
Clarendon Avenue
Leamington Spa
Warwickshire CV32 5PR

www.scholastic.co.uk

Printed by Bell and Bain Ltd, Glasgow

456789 456789012

**British Library Cataloguing-in-Publication
Data**
A catalogue record for this book is available from
the British Library.

ISBN 0-439-98481-5

Contents

 *Teacher's notes*    *Photocopiable*

Term 2

	N	P

Term 3

	N	P

N *Teacher's notes* P *Photocopiable*

Introduction

In *50 Shared texts* you will find a range of texts for use in shared reading. In recent years shared text work has become the focal point of daily literacy work, and the success of such shared work is clearly linked to the quality and choice of text. Better understanding of children's reading and writing development has led to the realisation that a greater range of text types, or genres, is needed to enrich children's literacy development. For the busy classroom teacher, seeking out such a range of quality texts can be too time-consuming, which is why appropriate texts have been provided in this book.

Shared reading

Shared reading is at the heart of the activities in this book and is a cornerstone of the National Literacy Strategy, which states that through shared reading children *begin to recognise important characteristics of a variety of written texts, often linked to style and voice.*

First developed in New Zealand by Don Holdaway, shared reading has been a significant literacy routine for children since the 1980s. Holdaway's research and pioneering work in schools brought the benefits of sharing enlarged texts or Big Books to teachers' attention. From his observations of very young children attending to bedtime stories on a one-to-one basis he realised that a similar intimacy with print could be offered through sharing an enlarged text with a group or class of children. He showed how engagement with Big Books can teach children about the characteristics of different text types, their organisation and distinguishing features, as well as the finer details of print. For example, depending on the teacher's focus, an enlarged recipe could be used at text level to model the way a piece of instructional writing is structured, at sentence level to look at the use of imperative verbs or at word level to focus on a particular phoneme. In relation to literature, the meaning of a poem can be explored at text level, the poet's choice

of verbs at sentence level and the rhyming pattern at word level. So, shared reading not only encourages the class to share the actual reading aloud of a text but also enables the teacher to discuss certain language features and support the children in both comprehending and responding to the text.

With younger children, shared reading involves following the text with a pointer to highlight key early concepts of print such as directionality and one-to-one correspondence. With such concepts securely in place, a rather different technique is needed for older children where the focus shifts more to understanding and responding to the text as well as discussing vocabulary and linguistic features. For all children, often the talk surrounding the reading is as important as the reading itself.

Finding the right quality texts for shared reading that will engage and interest the children, as well as meeting the many NLS objectives, can be a difficult task. Once a text is found, you need to identify salient features at word, sentence and text level.

Shared reading is also the springboard for shared writing, guided reading/writing and independent work. Both guided reading and writing provide opportunities for you to guide, support, model and comment on children's response to a text. Activities may involve reading aloud, role-play, performance or writing for a particular purpose. Independent activities may mirror these but need to be clearly structured to enable the children to work independently.

About this book

The texts in this book are organised term by term, following the NLS framework, so there are examples of fiction, poetry, plays and non-fiction.

For each text, both a blank and annotated version are provided. The former is for use with children and can either be enlarged or projected on an overhead projector; the latter is for teacher information and identifies the features of the text and links with NLS objectives.

Background

Background information is provided for each text. This will contextualise the extract, fill in any necessary details and give facts about its author as relevant. Information on themes, technical features or other related texts might also feature here.

Shared reading and discussing the text

This section offers guidance on ways of managing discussion around the text, as well as ways of organising the shared reading. Depending on the age of the children, and demands of the text, different strategies for working with the whole class on the text are given, as well as ways of triggering the children's responses. These include structured discussion suggestions, ideas for role-play, and performance techniques.

Activities

Building on the reading and discussion, this section suggests activities for both whole-class work and guided or independent group work. There are ideas for further textual analysis, sometimes involving shared writing. As in the previous section, talk is pivotal in developing the children's understanding.

Extension/further reading

Suggestions for taking activities into a broader context and ideas for linked reading are also provided, where appropriate. Reading may include books of the same genre, or texts that share the theme or the same author.

The texts

The choice of texts has been driven by the need to ensure that these are quality texts both in content and language. It is hoped that among the selection you will find a mixture of authors and texts, both familiar and new. Whole texts have been provided as far as possible so that children have the satisfaction of reading and appreciating a coherent and complete piece of writing.

Longer texts, such as novels, also need to feature in older children's reading, and sometimes more than one extract from the same carefully chosen novel has been included. Bearing in mind that children should experience as much of the novel as they can, it is recommended that you use the background notes to fill the children in on plot detail, and that you read the story to them or have copies, including a taped version, available for their own reading or listening. Other slots in the curriculum can be used for such reading: private reading, homework, independent group work or story time.

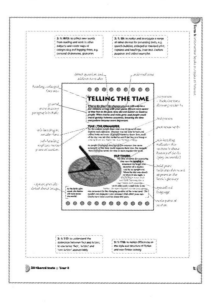

Range and objectives

Year 3 Term 1

Range	Text	NLS references
Stories with familiar settings	**'The Disastrous Dog'** from *Uninvited Ghosts* by Penelope Lively (Mammoth)	S2, T2, T6, T11
	'Esio Trot' from *Esio Trot* by Roald Dahl (Jonathan Cape)	S4, S5, T1, T3, T11, T16
	'A Sudden Puff of Glittering Smoke' from *A Sudden Puff of Glittering Smoke* by Anne Fine (Mammoth)	W8, S3, S4, S5, T1, T2
	'Cliffhanger' (extract 1) from *Cliffhanger* by Jacqueline Wilson (Corgi Yearling)	S2, S7, T2, T3
	'Cliffhanger' (extract 2) from *Cliffhanger* by Jacqueline Wilson (Corgi Yearling)	S2, S6, S7, S8, T2, T3, T10
Poems based on observation and the senses	**'The River'** by Valerie Bloom from *Spotlight on Poetry: Poems Around the World 3* edited by Brian Moses and David Orme (Collins Educational)	S1, T6, T7, T8
	'Trees Are Great' by Roger McGough from *Pillow Talk* (Puffin)	S6, T6, T8, T13
Shape poems	**'River'** and **'City River'** by June Crebbin from *Cows Moo, Cars Toot* by June Crebbin (Puffin)	W16, T6, T7, T8, T13, T14
	'Clouds' by Stanley Cook from *Madtail Miniwhale and Other Shape Poems* chosen by Wes Magee (Puffin)	W16, W18, T6, T7, T8, T13, T14
Playscripts	**'Sir Gawain and the Green Knight'** from *Sir Gawain and the Green Knight* by Steve Barlow and Steve Skidmore (Ginn & Co)	S2, S9, T4, T5, T15
	'Odysseus and the Cyclops' from *Odysseus and the Cyclops* by Paul Copley (Heinemann)	S2, S6, T3, T4, T5, T15
	'The Curse of the Baskervilles' from *The Pardoner's Tale and other plays* compiled by Irene Yates (Heinemann)	S2, S6, T3, T4, T5, T15
Information books on topics of interest	**'Wes Magee'** by Wes Magee (previously unpublished)	S9, T17, T18, T19, T21
	'Telling the time' from *Cycles in Science: Earth* by Peter D Riley (Heinemann Library)	W13, S9, T17, T18
Reports	**'How did the Vikings Live?'** from *The Vikings in Britain* by Robert Hull (Wayland)	W13, W14, S9, T17, T21
	'A new lemur discovered' from *Wildlife in the News* by John Craven and Mark Carwardine (Scholastic)	W13, W14, T21, T22, T23

Year 3 Term 2

Range	Text	NLS references
Myths and legends	**'King Midas'** from *The Orchard Book of Greek Myths* by Geraldine McCaughrean (Orchard Books)	T2, T3, T8, T9, T10
	'Odysseus' (extract 1) from *The Orchard Book of Greek Myths* by Geraldine McCaughrean (Orchard Books)	W12, S6, S7, T3, T6, T8, T10
	'Odysseus' (extract 2) from *The Orchard Book of Greek Myths* by Geraldine McCaughrean (Orchard Books)	S8, T2, T3, T8, T9, T10
Fables	**'The Miller, His Son and Their Donkey'** from *The Very Best of Aesop's Fables* by Margaret Clark (Walker Books)	T2, T3, T9, T10
	'The Boy Who Cried Wolf' from *The Very Best of Aesop's Fables* by Margaret Clark (Walker Books)	S4, T2, T8, T9
	'Three Raindrops' from *Fairy Tales and Fantastic Stories* by Terry Jones (Chrysalis Books)	S2, T2, T5, T6, T9
Traditional stories	**'The Greedy Man'** (extract 1) from *Moon Tales* by Rina Singh (Bloomsbury)	S2, S3, T1, T2, T8, T10
	'The Greedy Man' (extract 2) from *Moon Tales* by Rina Singh (Bloomsbury)	T1, T2, T8, T10
	'The Magic Porridge Pot' retold by Jackie Andrews (previously unpublished)	S2, S3, S6, T1, T9
	'The Story of the Mirror and its Fragments' from *The Snow Queen* by Hans Christian Andersen and PJ Lynch (Andersen Press)	S2, S3, T1, T3, T8, T9
Oral and performance poetry from different cultures	**'Tall Tales'** by Valerie Bloom from *Let Me Touch the Sky* by Valerie Bloom (Macmillan)	S2, S6, S8, T4, T5, T11
	'The Dragon Who Ate Our School' by Nick Toczek from *Dragons* by Nick Toczek (Macmillan Children's Books)	S6, S7, T4, T5, T11
	'The Boneyard Rap' by Wes Magee from *The Boneyard Rap and Other Poems* by Wes Magee (Hodder Wayland)	S6, S7, T4, T5, T11
	'Chicken Dinner' by Valerie Bloom from *Let Me Touch the Sky* by Valerie Bloom (Macmillan)	S1, T4, T5, T11
	'End of Term' (anon) from *I Saw Esau* by Iona Opie (Walker Books)	W17, W18, T4, T5, T11
Instructions	**'Nishnobblers'** from *Even More Revolting Recipes* by Roald Dahl (Jonathan Cape)	W17, S8, T12, T14, T15, T16
	'Shrimp' from *Underwater Origami* by Steve and Megumi Biddle (Red Fox)	T14, T15, T16

Year 3 Term 3

Range	Text	NLS references
Adventure and mystery stories	**'The Witch's Tears'** (extract 1) from *The Witch's Tears* by Jenny Nimmo (HarperCollins)	W13, S7, T2, T5, T11
	'The Witch's Tears' (extract 2) from *The Witch's Tears* by Jenny Nimmo (HarperCollins)	W13, T2, T5, T12
	'Clockwork' from *Clockwork* by Philip Pullman (Doubleday)	W11, W12, S4, T2, T3, T11, T12
	'Rosie's Zoo' from *Rosie's Zoo* by Ailie Busby (Scholastic)	S4, S6, T1, T10, T13
Stories by the same author	**'Horse Pie'** from *Horse Pie* by Dick King-Smith (Young Corgi)	W11, W13, S2, S4, S7, T2, T5, T8
	'The Guard-Dog' from *The Guard-Dog* by Dick King-Smith (Doubleday)	S1, S3, S4, S5, S6, T8, T9
	'The Finger-Eater' from *The Finger Eater* by Dick King-Smith (Walker Books)	W9, S2, S6, T2, T4, T5, T8
Humorous poetry	**'Monday's Child...'** (anon) and **'Monday's Child is Red and Spotty'** by Colin McNaughton from *The Hippo Book of Silly Poems* compiled by John Foster (Hippo)	W1, W2, W3, T6, T7
Poetry that plays with language	**'The Ceremonial Band'** by James Reeves from *Complete Poems for Children* by James Reeves (Heinemann Young Books)	W13, W14, S4, T7
	'Kennings' – **'Sun'** by Steve Turner from *The Day I Fell Down the Toilet and Other Poems* by Steve Turner (Lion Publishing) and **'Guess Who?'** by Coral Rumble from *The Works* chosen by Paul Cookson (Macmillan Children's Books)	W12, T6, T7, T15
Letters written for a range of purposes: to recount, to apologise	**'Wish You Were Here'** from *Wish You Were Here* by Martina Selway (Red Fox)	W2, W11, S6, T16, T19, T20, T21
	'The Jolly Postman' from *The Jolly Postman* by Janet and Allan Ahlberg (Puffin)	W5, T16, T20
Indexes	**'Subject Index'** from Northamptonshire County Council Libraries and Information Services	T17, T18
Explanations	**'How do seeds grow?'** from *Dig and Sow! How do plants grow?* by Janice Lobb (Kingfisher Books)	W14, T19, T21, T24
Alphabetic texts	**'Glossary'** from *Dig and Sow! How do plants grow?* by Janice Lobb (Kingfisher Books)	W12, T17, T24
Texts recounting the same event in a variety of ways	**'Henry's Secret Diary'** from *Dead Famous: Henry VIII and his Chopping Block* by Alan MacDonald and Philip Reeve (Scholastic)	W12, T3, T4, T5, T22
	'The Rise and Fall of the Mary Rose' by Sylvia Clements (previously unpublished)	T19, T22, T24, T25

The Disastrous Dog

by Penelope Lively

Background

The first five texts in this term come from four books by well-known authors. The stories all have settings with which the children will be familiar and characters that they might recognise, although the events in the story might be unexpected.

This first extract, from a short story by Penelope Lively, comes from a collection of animal stories and uses the popular idea of an animal that talks. The extract introduces the Roper family and their son Paul, who are visiting an animal sanctuary to select a dog. However, rather than them choosing a dog, unbeknown to them (apart from Paul) a rather nondescript brown mongrel selects them as his new owners. The dog, called Mick, has the ability to talk, but nobody in the family can hear him apart from Paul. Later on, the dog uses his unattractive and manipulative personality to get his own way. Paul soon longs for a speechless, dog-like dog, so, to everyone's relief, Mick is eventually returned to the Animal Sanctuary.

This slightly abridged extract comes from the beginning of the story and establishes the characters and their different reasons for wanting a dog.

Shared reading and discussing the text

● Read the first three sentences of the extract without showing the children the rest of the story. Discuss how they set the scene and warn the reader of trouble ahead. Then read the extract up until *dogs of all shapes and sizes*.

● Read the rest of the extract and ask the children what clues they can find about the dog's character, for example his abrupt manner of speaking and his description of the other dogs as an *ordinary mob*.

● Discuss with the children how they think the story might continue. Then tell them that the Roper family do take Mick home, but it does not turn out to be a success and he is eventually returned to the Sanctuary.

● Ask the children about the way the dialogue is presented in the extract, for example use of a new line for the start of each speech, use of speech marks and question marks, and so on. Point out to the children that when writing dialogue it is acceptable to write in the way people actually speak and not necessarily in complete sentences, for example *'Central heating? Garden?'*.

Activities

● Ask the children to think of different ways to adapt the first three sentences of the extract for their own story beginning.

● Discuss with the children why each member of the family wanted a dog from the Sanctuary. Put the children into groups of three and ask each child to take the role of one of the characters and say why he/she wants a dog.

● Give the children a two-column chart on which to record the contrast between the characteristics of the dog the family were looking for when they went to the Sanctuary and the dog they actually acquired.

● Ask the children to imagine what Mick will want to know when he arrives at the Ropers' home. For example, where is he going to sleep, what is he expected to eat? Tell the children to write a dialogue between Paul and Mick on arrival back home. Encourage them to use appropriate verbs and adverbs to indicate how the dialogue should be said. For example, Mick might demand loudly, snarl angrily or ask sullenly, while Paul might apologise quietly. Ask the children to read their dialogues in pairs with suitable expression.

Extension/further reading

Encourage the children to think about how being able to communicate with the demanding dog would have caused problems for Paul with his parents, who were oblivious. Ask them to write a dialogue in which Paul explains to his mother that he and Mick can talk to each other.

Stuart Little by EB White and *The Sam Pig Story Book* by Alison Uttley (both Puffin Books) continue the theme of talking animals.

3: 1: S2: to take account of the grammar and punctuation, e.g. sentences, speech marks, exclamation marks and commas to mark pauses, when reading aloud

3: 1: T2: how dialogue is presented in stories, e.g. through statements, questions, exclamations; how paragraphing is used to organise dialogue

short, incisive opening sentences achieve impact through repetition

italic used to stress word

2nd paragraph introduces and establishes the characters of the Roper family

adjectives and adverb contribute to this 1st description of the dog

instead of 'looked'; powerful verb creates impact

new line for each person speaking

confidential tone as narrator addresses reader

the characters' thoughts are described in a way that echoes their speech

capital letter for start of speech

use of speech marks

indicates speech is unfinished, he is interrupted

place to stay

suggests dog's manipulative and bossy character

curious

The Disastrous Dog

Some people buy dogs. Some people are given dogs. Some people are taken over by dogs, as you might say. I'll tell you what happened to the Ropers, just in case *your* parents ever decide to get a dog from the local Animal Sanctuary.

Mr Roper was in favour of getting a dog from the Sanctuary because he didn't see the point of paying good money for something when you can get it free. Mrs Roper thought it would be nice to give a home to a poor unwanted dog. Paul, who was nine, didn't really care where the dog came from so long as they had one. He'd been wanting a dog for ages, and now that they'd moved to a house down the end of a long lane, with no neighbours, outside the village, his father had come round to the idea. A guard dog, it was to be, a sensible efficient anti-burglar useful kind of dog.

The Animal Sanctuary seethed with dogs of all shapes and sizes…

…He looked at the dogs, carefully. They were all dashing around except for one, a nondescript brown animal with a stumpy tail and one white ear, which stood squarely beside the fence staring at Paul.

Paul glanced over at his parents; they were not looking in his direction. He stared back at the brown dog. "Did you say something?" he asked, feeling foolish.

"Too right I did," said the dog. "Do you live in a house or a flat?"

"A house. In the country."

"Central heating? Garden?"

"Yes. Listen, how come you…"

The dog interrupted. "Sounds a reasonable billet. Get your parents over here and I'll do my stuff. Homeless dog act. Never fails."

"Can they all?" asked Paul, waving at the other dogs. "Talk?"

The dog spluttered contemptuously. "Course not. Ordinary mob, that's all they are."

There was something not altogether attractive about the dog's personality, but Paul could not help being intrigued.

3: 1: T6: to discuss choice of words and phrases that describe and create impact, e.g. 'stare' instead of 'look'

3: 1: T11: to develop the use of settings in own stories by: writing short descriptions of known places; to investigate and collect sentences/ phrases for story openings and endings

Esio Trot

by Roald Dahl

Background

This extract comes from the beginning of *Esio Trot* – a story about a very shy man, Mr Hoppy, who is in love with Mrs Silver, a kind widow who lives in the flat below his, and the small tortoise Alfie who brings them together. In this extract, Roald Dahl introduces the very ordinary setting of a tall concrete block of flats and contrasts it with the beauty of Mr Hoppy's balcony filled with pots of colourful flowers.

Shared reading and discussing the text

● Read the extract up to the end of the third paragraph. Focus the children's attention on the words and phrases that describe the setting and underline these words. The children will discover that most of the description for the setting occurs in the first two paragraphs. Point out that many stories start by setting the scene and introducing the characters.

● Encourage the children to be aware that the story is being told by a narrator and is therefore written in the third person. Ask them why they think the narrator uses *I* at the end of the extract.

● The third paragraph states that Mr Hoppy's *second love was a secret he kept entirely to himself.* Discuss with the children what they think this second love might be.

● Now read the rest of the extract and ask the children what they have found out about the two characters. Point out how Roald Dahl portays the very ordinary lives of his characters, for example Mr Hoppy longs to invite Mrs Silver for a cup of tea and biscuit. Into this very everyday environment, Dahl uses the balcony for the exchange of conversation and therefore introduces the idea of romance associated with a balcony (as in *Romeo and Juliet*).

● Point out that the extract contains five paragraphs. Explain to the children that paragraphs can be of very different lengths, for example the third paragraph is only one sentence long. Why do they think this is? Focus the children's attention on the main topic for each paragraph.

● Explain to the children that the extract is written in the past tense, and underline the verbs in the first three paragraphs.

Activities

● Ask the children to imagine that they can hear the daily, polite conversation between Mr Hoppy and Mrs Silver. They should write this conversation down, remembering what they know about their characters (for example, they will probably talk about everyday things such as the weather, the flowers growing on the balcony and so on).

● Using a setting familiar to the children, for example the school nature garden or playground, build up a class word bank of appropriate vocabulary to describe it. Using this vocabulary, tell the children to write a description of the place. They should write this in the present tense, as they will find this easier initially.

● Ask the children to introduce one character, who can be real or imaginary, into their setting. Tell the children to write a brief character sketch for the person, using as models the ones for Mr Hoppy and Mrs Silver. Then tell the children to work in pairs and discuss how their two characters might meet.

● Tell the children to write down five or ten verbs from the passage and then change the tense, for example *say/saying/said.*

Extension/further reading

Ask the children as individuals to write a very precise description of a setting that they know well. Then working with a partner they read their description and their partner draws what they are told. The pairs then check how accurate the drawing is.

Explain that the story has a traditional 'happily every after' ending, with the two main characters being brought together by a tortoise, hence the title of the book, which is tortoise spelt backwards. Explore how the tortoise might have brought the characters together.

3: 1: S4: to use verb tenses with increasing accuracy in speaking and writing, e.g. *catch/caught, see/saw, go/went,* etc

3: 1: S5: to use the term 'verb' appropriately

3: 1: T1: to compare a range of story settings, and to select words and phrases that describe scenes

short, introductory paragraphs set the scene

1-sentence paragraph to build up suspense and emphasise importance of this 2nd love

3rd person narrator who knows things that characters don't

the narrator is the 'voice' of the story; we learn about characters through narrator's descriptions rather than dialogue

narrator intrudes on the action – an 'aside' to the reader

past tense verbs

allows the reader to infer that he is also a very patient man

emphasises the dichotomy between the very ordinary conversation and the romance associated with the balcony

reiterates Mr Hoppy's dilemma

Esio Trot

Mr Hoppy lived in a small flat high up in a tall concrete building. He lived alone. He had always been a lonely man and now that he was retired from work he was more lonely than ever.

There were two loves in Mr Hoppy's life. One was the flowers he grew on his balcony. They grew in pots and tubs and baskets, and in summer the little balcony became a riot of colour.

Mr Hoppy's second love was a secret he kept entirely to himself.

The balcony immediately below Mr Hoppy's jutted out a good bit further from the building than his own, so Mr Hoppy always had a fine view of what was going on down there. This balcony belonged to an attractive middle-aged lady called Mrs Silver. Mrs Silver was a widow who also lived alone. And although she didn't know it, it was she who was the object of Mr Hoppy's secret love. He had loved her from his balcony for many years, but he was a very shy man and he had never been able to bring himself to give her even the smallest hint of his love.

Every morning, Mr Hoppy and Mrs Silver exchanged polite conversation, the one looking down from above, the other looking up, but that was as far as it ever went. The distance between their balconies might not have been more than a few yards, but to Mr Hoppy it seemed like a million miles. He longed to invite Mrs Silver up for a cup of tea and a biscuit, but every time he was about to form the words on his lips, his courage failed him. As I said, he was a very very shy man.

3: 1: T3: to be aware of the different voices in stories using dramatised readings, showing differences between the narrator and different characters used

3: 1: T11: to develop the use of settings in own stories by:
● writing short descriptions of known places
● writing a description in the style of a familiar story

3: 1: T16: to begin to organise stories into paragraphs; to begin to use paragraphing in presentation of dialogue in stories

A Sudden Puff of Glittering Smoke by Anne Fine

Background

This extract is taken from a story set in the familiar environment of a school. Into this everyday setting, Anne Fine introduces magic in the form of a disgruntled genie who has been stuck in a ring for 500 years. Only visible to the wearer of the ring, the genie appears to Jeanie at school to fulfil all her commands and wishes. In the end, Jeanie finds out that the genie and his magic are a whole lot more trouble than they are worth and she gives the ring away.

Shared reading and discussing the text

● Read the first paragraph together. Ask the children where this story is set. How do they know?

● Now finish the extract. Ask the children to identify the turning point and to find key words that describe the dramatic turn of events.

● Ask the children what they notice about the girl's name and *genie*. Make sure they appreciate the wordplay if they have not already spotted it.

● Anne Fine uses the familiar setting of a school to introduce magic and the unexpected. Point out to the children the dramatic language Anne Fine uses to announce the arrival of the genie.

● Read the paragraph describing the genie again and look closely at the vocabulary used to build up an exotic description of the genie. Discuss with the children what their image of a genie might be and ask what other stories they have read with the character of a genie in them, for example 'Aladdin'.

● Point out to the children how dialogue is presented in the extract and focus on the genie's actions of folding his arms and bowing and his first word, *'Greetings'*, which is a very traditional way for a genie to behave in stories. Explain that this is going to be important for a drama activity.

● Focus the children's attention on the way Anne Fine has varied the length of her paragraphs and discuss why she made *It was a genie* into a paragraph on its own (to emphasise the importance of the statement).

● Highlight one or two of the verbs in the text that end in *-ing*, for example *spinning*. Point out how the spelling of the verb changes when the *-ing* is removed.

Activities

● Tell the children to re-read the description of the genie and highlight effective words and phrases. They can then go on to write a description of their *own* genie after building up a class word bank of suitable vocabulary. Encourage them to think about how the genie will appear, how he will be dressed, his size.

● Ask the children to work in pairs to write several questions they would like to ask their genie. They can then take it in turns to ask and answer the questions in role.

● Ask the children to decide how they will make their genie appear. This might be in the traditional way of rubbing a lamp or by saying a special word, or in a less controlled way, for example every time there was a storm or rain. They should record their ideas in writing.

● Explain to the children that they are going to be the narrator of a story about their genie, and ask them to write two or three paragraphs as an opening. Prompt them to set the story in a familiar environment, such as a classroom, and to describe the setting. They can then introduce a character, such as a Year 3 child.

● Ask the children to identify five to ten verbs in the text that end in *-ing*. Ask them to write down the verbs without the *-ing*. They could then use a thesaurus to find alternative verbs.

Extension/further reading

Working in pairs, ask the children to read their description of a genie to their partner, who must draw as accurately as possible what they have been told.

Philip Pullman retells the story of Aladdin and the genie in *The Wonderful Story of Aladdin and the Enchanted Lamp* (Scholastic). A more traditional retelling is *Aladdin and other tales for the Arabian nights* edited by NJ Dawood (Puffin).

3: 1: W8: how the spellings of verbs alter when -*ing* is added

3: 1: S3: the function of verbs in sentences through:
● noticing that sentences cannot make sense without them
● collecting and classifying examples of verbs from reading and own knowledge
● experimenting with changing simple verbs in sentences and discussing their impact on meaning

3: 1: S4: to use verb tenses with increasing accuracy in speaking and writing, e.g. *catch/caught, see/saw, go/went*, etc. Use past tense consistently for narration

vocabulary establishes school setting

A Sudden Puff of Glittering Smoke

Jeanie sat at her desk, twisting the ring on her finger round and round. The ring was bothering her terribly. It was so tight she couldn't get it off. She'd only found it a couple of hours before, glinting so brightly in the gutter she was astonished no one else had noticed it. She'd picked it up and looked around, wondering what to do. Then, when the school bell rang, she'd pushed it hastily onto a finger and run the last few yards into the playground.

But in her hurry she had shoved it on the wrong finger. Now she'd been struggling with it all through register.

"Call out your name if you are having a school dinner today," ordered Mr Piper.

"David!"

"Asha!"

"William!"

"Jeanie!"

As she called out her name, she couldn't help giving the ring another little twist.

There was a sudden puff of glittering smoke, and the ring was spinning on the desk in front of her. Jeanie drew her hand away smartly, and stared in wonder.

Before her eyes, the smoke turned to a column of glistening fog, then formed a spinning ball, then took – slowly, slowly – a strange and ancient shape.

It was a genie.

No doubt about it. He was no taller than her pencil and mist still curled around him; but he looked like every genie she had ever seen in books: a little fat in the belly, with a silk bodice and billowing pantaloons that looked for all the world as if they had been woven from silver shifting mists. Tiny stars winked all over them, and they were held up by a belt of pure gold. On his feet were the tiniest curly slippers, with pointed ends.

Folding his arms, the genie bowed low.

"Greetings," he said.

opening paragraph sets the scene in a school

short paragraph with 2 sentences

verb, present participle of 'struggle'

present participle of verb 'spin' (used adjectivally)

sounds like 'Jeanie'

moving in large waves

baggy trousers fastened just above the ankle

verb, present participle of 'twist'

the dash emphasises the slowness of the action

descriptive device: comparison

descriptive device: adjectives

descriptive device: personification

3: 1: S5: to use the term 'verb' appropriately

3: 1: T1: to compare a range of story settings, and to select words and phrases that describe scenes

3: 1: T2: how dialogue is presented in stories, e.g. through statements, questions, exclamations; how paragraphing is used to organise dialogue

Cliffhanger

by Jacqueline Wilson

Extract 1

Background

Tim is hopeless at sport. His father is keen for him to go on an adventure holiday, while his mother is very protective and thinks the holiday sounds far too dangerous. Once at the adventure centre, Tim's initial reluctance and fears give way as he gains confidence and respect by helping his team to win a game. This first extract, which comes from the beginning of the book, clearly establishes the very different characters of Tim's parents and the tensions between them. It also demonstrates Tim's passive role in contributing to discussions and decisions within the family. Tim narrates the story, so the reader is aware of his feelings although he is unable to express these to his arguing parents.

Shared reading and discussing the text

● Read as far as the first *I went on watching telly*. Ask the children what we already know about Tim's mum and dad. Ask them who is telling the story.

● Now finish reading the extract and encourage the children to comment on how they think Tim is feeling while his parents discuss his possible visit to the adventure centre. Ask the children to find the parts of the extract that help to make clear Tim's feelings, for example *my heart had started thumping under my T-shirt*.

● Divide the class in half. In pairs, one half discuss Dad's reasons for wanting Tim to go and the other half discuss Mum's reservations. Share their ideas.

● Ask the children what we know about Tim's favourite activities and what the adventure centre offers. The contrast between these two gives the reader a clue that there are going to be some problems for Tim.

● Focus attention on the dialogue and how it is presented. Explain that dialogue is used in this extract to give an indication of the characters of Tim's parents. Reinforce the rules for the use of punctuation within speech marks.

● Look at the number of times *said* is used and encourage the children to think of alternative words. Build up a class word bank of synonyms.

Activities

● Invite three children to read the extract to the class. Allocate the most fluent reader to read Tim's part as the narrator. The other two children take on the roles of Dad and Mum. Encourage them to read with expression. If there were enough adults in the room or very confident readers it would help to give a demonstration.

● Follow this up in guided group work, giving more children the chance to re-enact the passage. Then tell the children to continue the dialogue between the three characters. Focus on using the correct punctuation for all speech, and encourage them to use a variety of words to explain how each comment is made, for example *demanded Dad, encouraged Mum*.

● Explain to the children that Tim does go to the adventure centre, and ask them to write two or three paragraphs about how he might feel when he arrives.

● Ask the children to design and write a postcard from Tim to his parents when he is first at the adventure centre. Point out to the children that it would be an unhappy message as Tim was so reluctant to go on the adventure holiday and would not have had time to make friends or start to feel confident about the activities.

Extension/further reading

The extract is written from Tim's point of view. Ask the children to write part of the first chapter from the point of view of either Tim's father or mother, explaining their motive for wanting their son to go or not to go on the holiday.

Other Jacqueline Wilson books, such as *The Suitcase Kid* (Corgi Childrens), portray children and their emotions in difficult situations.

opening paragraphs explain clearly Tim's attitude and thoughts

narrated in the 1st person

indication of how Tim sees his father's character

unfinished sentence

reveals Mum's protective nature

Tim is silent for most of the conversation although his parents are talking about him

short, snappy sentences quicken pace

conventions of speech punctuation: speech marks then capital letter, comma before closing speech marks

Cliffhanger

Extract 1

I knew I'd hate it. I kept telling and telling Dad. But he wouldn't listen to me. He never does.

"I like the sound of this adventure holiday for children," said Dad, pointing to the advert in the paper. "Abseiling, canoeing, archery, mountain biking. . ."

"Sounds a bit dangerous to me," said Mum.

I didn't say anything. I went on watching telly.

"How about it, Tim?" said Dad. "What about an adventure holiday, eh?"

"You can't be serious! Tim's much too young," said Mum.

I still didn't say anything. I went on watching telly. But my heart had started thumping under my T-shirt.

"He's nine, for goodness sake!" said Dad.

"But he's young for his age," said Mum.

I still didn't say anything. I went on watching telly. I stared hard at the screen, wishing there was some way I could step inside.

"Tim?" said Dad.

I didn't look round quickly enough.

"Tim! Stop watching television!" Dad shouted.

I jumped.

"Don't shout at him like that," said Mum.

"I'm not shouting," Dad shouted. He took a deep breath. He turned his lips up into a big smile. "Now, Tim — you'd like to go on an adventure holiday, wouldn't you?"

"He'd hate it," said Mum.

"Let him answer for himself," said Dad. He had hold of me by the shoulders.

"I – I don't really like adventures much, Dad," I said.

Dad went on smiling, but I think he wanted to give my shoulders a shake.

"Well, what do you like, Tim?" asked Dad.

"Watching telly," I said.

Dad snorted.

"And drawing and reading and doing puzzles," said Mum. "And he comes top in all his lessons at school. Apart from games. You know he's hopeless at sport."

"Only because he doesn't give it a try," said Dad.

repetition of 'said'

reveals how Tim is feeling

emphasises Tim's strong wish to escape from the situation

build-up of tension between Tim and his father

stronger verb after repetition of 'said'

he is shouting!

threatening action

question mark before closing speech marks

Cliffhanger

by Jacqueline Wilson

Extract 2

Background

In this second extract from *Cliffhanger*, Tim is reluctantly being encouraged to try abseiling. Jake, the group leader, is attempting to be very reassuring, but Tim is not convinced and the extract ends with Tim suspended in mid-air. Tension is built up through the piece by a combination of short exchanges, Jake's repeated instructions and hints of Tim's increasing panic.

Shared reading and discussing the text

● Tell the children that this second extract from *Cliffhanger* starts when Tim is at the adventure centre and is attempting to take his turn at abseiling. Ask the children if they know what this is and why it can be scary. Tell the children about the characters in this extract: Jake – the group leader who is very kind and supportive to Tim; Biscuits – a friend Tim has made on the holiday who is very fond of food; Giles – another child who is very confident and good at sport and is not supportive of Tim.

● Read the extract. Then go through it again, asking the children how they think Tim is feeling at different points. For example, Tim feels he has no way out of the situation because Jake does not agree when he says '*No!*'.

● Focus the children's attention on how the dialogue is presented in the extract, looking at speech marks, capital letters, question marks and exclamation marks. Look at Jake's encouraging comments and actions and compare them with Tim's short replies, for example '*No!*' and '*Later*'.

● Explain that the extract ends at a very dramatic point and discuss with the children what they think might happen next. Tell them that the drama and suspense is built up by the use of punctuation, for example *suddenly... there I was*, exclamation marks, a one-word sentence *Suspended*, and the paragraph ending with Tim in mid-air.

● Discuss what the children think might happen next in the story, and then tell them that Tim does complete the abseiling task successfully.

● Although the passage describes a distressing incident, it does include a lot of humour. Can the children pinpoint the phrases that contribute to the humour? For example, *personalized helmet* (he probably doesn't look very cool!) and '*Open your eyes!*' (after he thought that closing his eyes might help).

Activities

● Tell the children to continue the dialogue between Tim and Jake. Jake will have to encourage Tim not to panic and keep hold of the rope.

● Ask the children to write about how Tim might feel after completing the abseiling task.

● Ask the children to imagine they are Tim and are now enjoying the adventure holiday. Encourage them to think of an activity they would enjoy, for example canoeing, archery, mountain biking, swimming, horse riding and to write a postcard home as Tim, explaining how much they enjoyed the activity.

● Ask each child to write a dialogue between themselves and a friend who is scared to tackle the activity they chose to write about above. How would they encourage their friend? In pairs, the children can read their dialogue using appropriate expression.

Extension/further reading

Ask the children to design a brochure for an activity holiday that explains the activities offered, describes the centre's location, includes a diagram on how to reach it and what the accommodation is like. Remind them that they are trying to encourage children to visit, so it must appeal to parents, who may be concerned with safety issues, as well as children, who will want fun activities.

Provide the children with copies of *Cliffhanger* to read the rest of the story. There is also a video available of *Cliffhanger* made by Channel 4 Schools.

Children will enjoy reading other Jacqueline Wilson books, such as *The Story of Tracy Beaker* and *The Lottie Project* (Corgi Childrens).

3: 1: S2: to take account of the grammar and punctuation, e.g. sentences, speech marks, exclamation marks and commas to mark pauses, when reading aloud

3: 1: S6: to secure knowledge of question marks and exclamation marks in reading, understand their purpose and use appropriately in own writing

3: 1: S7: the basic conventions of speech punctuation through:
● identifying speech marks in reading
● beginning to use in own writing
● using capital letters to mark the start of direct speech

Cliffhanger

Extract 2

"OK, Tim. You next."

"No!"

"Yes," said Jake, coming over to me.

"No," I said.

"You've all got to go sooner or later," said Jake.

"Later," I insisted.

"No. Sooner," said Jake. "Get it over with."

"I can't," I said.

"Yes you can, Tim," said Jake, holding my hand.

"He's scared," said Giles.

"We all get scared," said Jake. "Especially the first time." He bent down and looked me straight in the eye. "But you'll see it's easy, Tim. Trust me. Now. Into the harness."

I found I was being strapped in before I could get away. Jake was telling me things about this rope in this hand, that rope in that, but the wind was whipping his words away. I couldn't listen properly anyway. There was just this roaring inside my head.

"Don't let go of the rope, right?" said Jake.

I felt as if my head was going to burst right out of my personalized safety helmet.

This couldn't be real. It couldn't be happening to me. If I closed my eyes maybe it would all turn into a nightmare and then I'd wake up in bed at home with Walter Bear.

"Tim?" said Jake. "Open your eyes! Now, your pal Biscuits is down there waiting for you. Come on. Start backing towards the edge."

I backed one step. Then another. Then I stopped.

"I can't!"

"Yes you can," said Jake. "You'll see. Over you go. Don't worry. You can't fall. You just have to remember, you *don't* let go of the rope."

I stared at him and started backing some more. Then my heels suddenly lost contact with the ground. I slipped backwards and suddenly... there I was! Suspended. In mid-air.

short, repetitive exchange builds up tension

strap to support person during abseiling

build-up of tension

use of short sentences to heighten tension

Tim's teddy bear who was left at home

Tim still not listening properly

gradual build-up of suspense with punctuation

important instructions

Tim's fear is preventing him listening to Jake's instructions

dramatic effect of wind

Tim's mum had written his name on his helmet

1-word sentence for dramatic effect

3: 1: S8: to use the term 'speech marks'

3: 1: T2: how dialogue is presented in stories, e.g. through statements, questions, exclamations; how paragraphing is used to organise dialogue

3: 1: T3: to be aware of the different voices in stories using dramatised readings, showing differences between the narrator and different characters used

3: 1: T10: using reading as a model, to write own passages of dialogue

The River

by Valerie Bloom

Background

This poem and the following one encourage children to focus on the five senses (sight/touch/taste/smell/hearing) to interpret the world around them and to record these observations in a sensitive and structured way.

Valerie Bloom was born in Jamaica and came to live in England in 1979. She believes it is very important to be acutely aware of everything around you for ideas for writing and that it is essential to use your senses for this. This poem has a reassuring sense of pattern with the repeated phrase *The River's a...* providing the children with a structure to use in their own writing. Each verse is an extended metaphor and good use is made of personification to explain the river's actions and moods, helping children access the meaning of the poem.

Shared reading and discussing the text

● After modelling reading the poem, ensure that the children understand that each verse is an extended metaphor. Go through the first verse unpicking the metaphor.
● Ask the children what trick the poet has used to describe the river vividly. If they are unsure, ask them what they would expect a *tramp* to be (a person). Look together at the personification devices Bloom has used in the first verse. Ask the children, in pairs, to seek out other examples in the rest of the poem, for example the initial capital in *River.*
● Focus the children's attention on the choice of vocabulary, for example *nomad*, *hoarder* and *vexed* and discuss their meanings in the poem.
● Discuss the pattern of the poem having four lines in each verse and the repetition of *The River's a...* to start each verse. What do the children notice about the pattern of the rhymes in each verse? Explain that the rhythm and sound of the poem is an important feature.
● What *treasures* do the children think the river has buried down deep? Explain that the river's idea of what constitutes treasure might not be the same as theirs.
● Read the poem again to remind the children

how the pattern and ideas fit together. Display an enlarged copy in the classroom (poems can become more enjoyable when they are familiar).
● In pairs, ask the children which verse they liked best and why. They can then practise reciting their favourite verses together.

Activities

● In pairs, ask the children to suggest other nouns to add to the first line, for example *The River's a snake/provider/giant/seeker.*
● Choose one of the words the children have selected in the above activity and model writing another verse for the poem, explaining how and particularly emphasising your choice of verbs. Perhaps make your river female:

> The River's a snake
> She glides smoothly along
> Forked tongue flicking
> Singing her own song.

● Emphasise the use of rhyme on the second and fourth lines of each verse. In group work, children could label and list all the rhyming pairs of words. They could add to this, using a rhyming dictionary to find more words.
● Ask the children to write one or more verses using the same pattern as Valerie Bloom. Ask them to read out their verses and combine these to make a class poem – each child writing out and illustrating their own verse.

Extension/further reading

Select another subject, such as 'The Tree' or 'The Earth', and ask the children to write a poem using the same structure as 'The River'.

Look at collections of poems by Valerie Bloom, such as *Let Me Touch the Sky* (Macmillan Children's Books) and *The World is Sweet* (Bloomsbury Children's Books). Look at other poems that make central use of personification as a device, such as 'Autumn' by TE Hulme and 'Birds' by I Rawnsely, both of which can be found in *This Poem Doesn't Rhyme*, edited by Gerard Benson (Puffin Books).

3: 1: S1: to use awareness of grammar to decipher new or unfamiliar words, e.g. to predict from the text, read on, leave a gap and return; to use these strategies in conjunction with knowledge of phonemes, word recognition, graphic knowledge and context when reading

3: 1: T6: to read aloud and recite poems, comparing different views of the same subject; to discuss choice of words and phrases that describe and create impact, e.g. adjectives, powerful and expressive verbs, e.g. 'stare' instead of 'look'

repeated phrase giving structure to poem

personification devices: capitalised initial, nouns normally used to describe people, pronoun 'he'

use of capital letters at beginning of each line – poetic device

The River

The River's a wanderer,
A nomad, a tramp,
He never chooses one place
To set up his camp.

The River's a winder, a
Through valley and hill b
He twists and he turns c
He just cannot be still. b

The River's a hoarder
And he buries down deep
Those little treasures
That he wants to keep.

The River's a baby,
He gurgles and hums,
And sounds like he's happily
Sucking his thumbs.

The River's a singer,
As he dances along,
The countryside echoes
The notes of his song.

The River's a monster
Hungry and vexed,
He's gobbled up trees
And he'll swallow you next.

Valerie Bloom

extended metaphor

rhyming pattern: ABCB

vocabulary may be unfamiliar; note possibilities for inference here

expressive verbs to support metaphor of river as a baby

may need explanation; note word rhymes with 'next'

expressive verbs for a raging river

3: 1: T7: to distinguish between rhyming and non-rhyming poetry and comment on the impact of layout

3: 1: T8: to express their views about a story or poem, identifying specific words and phrases to support their viewpoint

Trees Are Great

by Roger McGough

P
116

Background

Roger McGough was born in Liverpool and his first career was as a teacher, but he soon left this to become a professional singer/actor and poet. He believes that it is the act of writing that stimulates his imagination and he particularly enjoys condensing thought and making word patterns and rhyme. This emphasis on rhyme and pattern is what makes this poem especially suitable to use with children. McGough enjoys using humour in his poems and examples of this can be seen in a line such as *Where would we hang the leaves?* This poem also uses examples of personification to help the reader understand the ideas he wishes to express.

Shared reading and discussing the text

● Read the poem, then ask the children to listen to it again and decide which line they enjoyed most.
● If they have not commented on the humour, ask the children whether they think McGough has tried to write a serious or a funny poem. They should find examples from the poem to back up their answers.
● Ask the children to identify words they are unsure of, for example *congregate*, *fate*. Explain that it is often possible to guess what a word means by reading on. For example in the case of *congregate*, the next line gives a clue when it includes *for meetings*.
● Remind the children about Valerie Bloom's use of personification in 'The River' (see page 20). What do they notice about this poem? Identify a few examples together.
● Explore the pattern of rhyme in the poem. The children may see the rhyme on the second and fourth lines of the first three verses, for example *teased/pleased* and *park/dark*. Encourage them to find the internal rhyme in the first lines of each verse, for example *great/wait* and *great/congregate*. What other rhymes would work in these cases? Record the children's suggestions so that these could be displayed and used later for writing additional verses.

Activities

● Using the words *Trees are great*, model writing an additional verse for the poem:

> Trees are great, they are never late
> For any appointment you might make
> They are always there when you plan to meet
> Your best friend for a date.

● Ask the children to write their own additional verse. Provide them with rhyming dictionaries or class examples of rhyming words.
● Ask the children to look at the last verse and the questions it raises. Encourage them to think of additional lines, such as *Where would apples grow? Where would squirrels play?* Ask the children to write down the first line of this verse and then add their own lines of questions.
● Working independently, children can highlight all the examples of personification they can find. They could then use these lists to generate synonyms, for example *wail/sob*.
● Using another subject for the first line, for example *Water is great, Elephants are great* and so on, ask the children to write their own poem using the same format. They could also end it with a range of questions in the last verse. It could be copied out for handwriting practice.
● Children could make sketches of any suitable large tree or trees in the school grounds or nearby, and use these to illustrate their poems. Visits could be made at different times of the year to encourage a different response, for example a place for shade in summer, branches for snow to sit on in winter.

Extension/further reading

Children could read other poems about trees from the anthology *Twinkle, Twinkle, Planet Blue* edited by Morag Styles (CUP). Roger McGough has written a number of poetry books including *Bad Bad Cats* and *An Imaginary Menagerie* (both Puffin). Another Liverpool poet is Brian Patten, who has written *Gargling with Jelly* and *Juggling with Gerbils*, also published by Puffin.

3: 1: S6: to secure knowledge of question marks and exclamation marks in reading, understand their purpose and use appropriately in own writing

3: 1: T6: to read aloud and recite poems, comparing different views of the same subject; to discuss choice of words and phrases that describe and create impact, e.g. adjectives, powerful and expressive verbs, e.g. 'stare' instead of 'look'

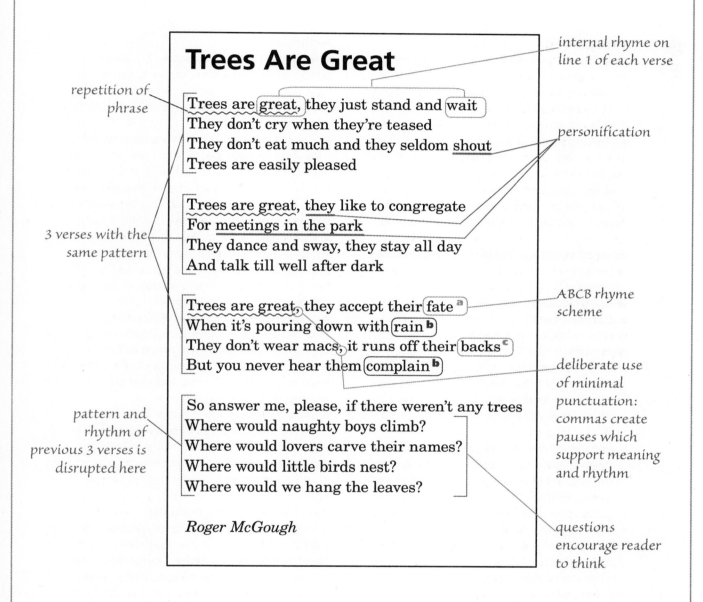

internal rhyme on line 1 of each verse

repetition of phrase

personification

3 verses with the same pattern

ABCB rhyme scheme

pattern and rhythm of previous 3 verses is disrupted here

deliberate use of minimal punctuation: commas create pauses which support meaning and rhythm

questions encourage reader to think

Trees Are Great

Trees are great, they just stand and wait
They don't cry when they're teased
They don't eat much and they seldom shout
Trees are easily pleased

Trees are great, they like to congregate
For meetings in the park
They dance and sway, they stay all day
And talk till well after dark

Trees are great, they accept their fate [a]
When it's pouring down with rain [b]
They don't wear macs, it runs off their backs [c]
But you never hear them complain [b]

So answer me, please, if there weren't any trees
Where would naughty boys climb?
Where would lovers carve their names?
Where would little birds nest?
Where would we hang the leaves?

Roger McGough

3: 1: T8: to express their views about a story or poem, identifying specific words and phrases to support their viewpoint

3: 1: T13: to collect suitable words and phrases, in order to write poems and short descriptions; design simple patterns with words, use repetitive phrases; write imaginative comparisons

River and City River

by June Crebbin

Background

These poems both take the shape of a river and are made up of a list of descriptive compound phrases, or 'kennings'. The use of kennings dates back to Viking times. Here, a modern poet uses the device to capture and compare the very different qualities of a rural and an urban river. The lines are short and crisp (encouraging for children who find pages of print a challenge) and the structure of each poem is the same – each line comprising two words joined by a hyphen. This is the only punctuation used.

Shared reading and discussing the text

● Conceal the titles of the poems before reading both through together.
● Ask the children what they think the titles of the poems might be and why.
● Now, working in pairs, ask the children what they notice about how the poet has described the rivers. Try to elicit the following:
  – the use of personification with which they should be familiar having worked on 'The River' (page 20) and 'Trees Are Great' (page 22)
  – the way the layout of the poems has been shaped to resemble the curves and meandering of a river (if they do not already know, tell them this is a 'shape poem')
  – the use of two-word phrases to describe the river, which do not contain the word *river* (introduce the word *kenning* if you feel it is appropriate)
  – the use of alliteration.
Ask the children to seek out further examples of personification, alliteration and kennings.
● Identify one of the 'pairs' of contrasting lines across the poems, for example *bank-lapper* and *wall-slapper*. Can the children find any more?
● Ask the children which of the two poems they prefer and why. They should select favourite words or phrases to justify their choices.

Activities

● Ask the children to work on preparing performances of each poem in guided or independent group work. Alternatively, they can work in pairs, reading the poems to each other.
● Children can record six key words they think work best in each poem and then go on to think of synonyms or suitable alternatives for these. For example, *tree* in *tree-reflector* could be replaced with *cloud*. You may wish to provide them with thesauruses for this activity.
● In shared writing, ask the children to contribute lines to a river poem based on a river in the school's vicinity. A visit to the river would help the creative process, especially if sketches and photographs were included.
● Choose either the country or city environment most accessible to the school and ask the children to write their own poems in the same style as June Crebbin's. They should then write them out as shape poems, focusing on layout and handwriting.
● Choose another topic and write a poem in the same style. Suggested topics could be 'the sea' or 'giants'. Write down all the objects with which the subject comes into contact and then how it touches them.

Extension/further reading

Select and read another poem about rivers with the children. Other, very different, poems about rivers include 'Where Go the Boats' by Robert Louis Stevenson from *A Child's Garden of Verses*, 'Reedy River' by Henry Lawson from the *Walker Book of Classic Poetry and Poets* selected by Michael Rosen and 'The River is a Piece of Sky' by John Giardi from *Young Puffin Book of Verse* by Barbara Ivesen.

The children could make a class anthology of poems and artwork based on the theme of rivers.

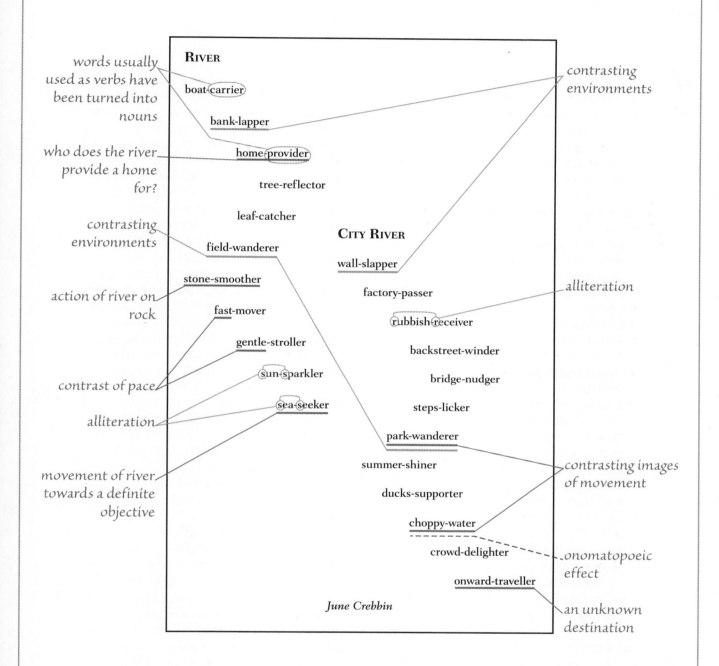

3: 1: W16: to understand the purpose and organisation of the thesaurus, and to make use of it to find synonyms

3: 1: T6: to read aloud and recite poems, comparing different views of the same subject; to discuss choice of words and phrases that describe and create impact, e.g. adjectives, powerful and expressive verbs, e.g. 'stare' instead of 'look'

3: 1: T7: to distinguish between rhyming and non-rhyming poetry and comment on the impact of layout

words usually used as verbs have been turned into nouns

who does the river provide a home for?

contrasting environments

action of river on rock

contrast of pace

alliteration

movement of river towards a definite objective

RIVER

boat-carrier

bank-lapper

home-provider

tree-reflector

leaf-catcher

field-wanderer

stone-smoother

fast-mover

gentle-stroller

sun-sparkler

sea-seeker

CITY RIVER

wall-slapper

factory-passer

rubbish-receiver

backstreet-winder

bridge-nudger

steps-licker

park-wanderer

summer-shiner

ducks-supporter

choppy-water

crowd-delighter

onward-traveller

June Crebbin

contrasting environments

alliteration

contrasting images of movement

onomatopoeic effect

an unknown destination

3: 1: T8: to express their views about a story or poem, identifying specific words and phrases to support their viewpoint

3: 1: T13: to collect suitable words and phrases, in order to write poems and short descriptions; design simple patterns with words, use repetitive phrases; write imaginative comparisons

3: 1: T14: to invent calligrams and a range of shape poems, selecting appropriate words and careful presentation. Build up class collections

Clouds

by Stanley Cook

Background

Shape poems offer an exciting mix of the visual and verbal and provide children with a new way of experiencing poetry. A shape poem takes the form of its subject matter. A calligram uses individual words shaped to resemble their subject. In both types of poem, pictures and words become interchangeable, with pictures becoming poems and poems becoming pictures. A tree can grow from one word, a balloon float away or words can even climb a mountain in a shape poem.

'Clouds' uses an exciting range of metaphors and rhyming couplets that will hopefully encourage children to add their own lines and find inspiration for poems about other subjects.

Shared reading and discussing the text

● Start by reading the poem to the children without showing them the text at all. Now put a copy of the poem on the OHP and allow the children a few minutes to look at it silently. Ask them why they think you read it *to* them first.

● Ask the children which image in the poem they enjoyed the most and encourage them to give a reason for their choice.

● Ask them to identify words they do not understand and discuss in pairs what they think their meanings could be, for example *white shrouds, unfurled* and *archipelago*.

● As well as the shaping of the poem, what other poetic devices can the children identify (for example, personification)?

Activities

● Select some of the words from the poem, such as *gigantic, airy* and *mountainously*, and encourage the children to think of synonyms for these words. When they have made an effort to find alternative words, let them use a thesaurus to add further to their list.

● Ask the children if they can find the rhymes in the poem, and write these down. Encourage them to add words of their own to these rhyming groups and share these with the class.

● Tell the children to add two or more couplets to the poem, encouraging them to use rhyming words at the end of the lines. Ask the children to read aloud the lines they have added and use these to construct a new class poem.

● Tell the children to write out the poem, creating their own shape as their response to the images in the poem. Then ask them to add their own lines as a handwriting exercise.

● Select another subject, such as trees or a musical instrument, and ask the children to brainstorm words associated with it. They could use a thesaurus to extend their range of words. Ask them to contribute their words to a class list and then encourage them to add rhyming words to this list. Now, ask individuals to write two or more rhyming couplets about the subject, using the list. These lines could be read out to the class and then incorporated into a class shape poem.

● Now, ask the children to draw an outline for their own poem making it as big as their page. They could start by using the lines they have already written or you could select two different opening lines. The children then continue to add their own lines and the finished work could be presented in a class book.

Extension/further reading

Introduce the idea that poems do not always need to start at the top of the page, for example a poem based on the idea of climbing stairs could start at the bottom. Tell the children to draw ten or more stairs and then imagine they are climbing them into a dark and scary place. Ask them to write a line for each stair, becoming scarier the higher they go. The poem could have a humorous ending on the top stair, for example when Mum switches the light on.

Look at other shape poems in Wes Magee's *Madtail, Miniwhale and Other Shape Poems* (Puffin Books). In *Nibbling the Page*, also selected by Wes Magee (Longman), there are a number of excellent examples of shape poems, for example 'Sixteen Steps to the Ice House' by Gina Douthwaite and 'Lark' by Leonard Clark.

3: 1: W16: to understand the purpose and organisation of the thesaurus, and to make use of it to find synonyms

3: 1: T6: to read aloud and recite poems, comparing different views of the same subject; to discuss choice of words and phrases that describe and create impact, e.g. adjectives, powerful and expressive verbs, e.g. 'stare' instead of 'look'

3: 1: T7: to distinguish between rhyming and non-rhyming poetry and comment on the impact of layout

3: 1: W18: to use the term 'synonym'

CLOUDS

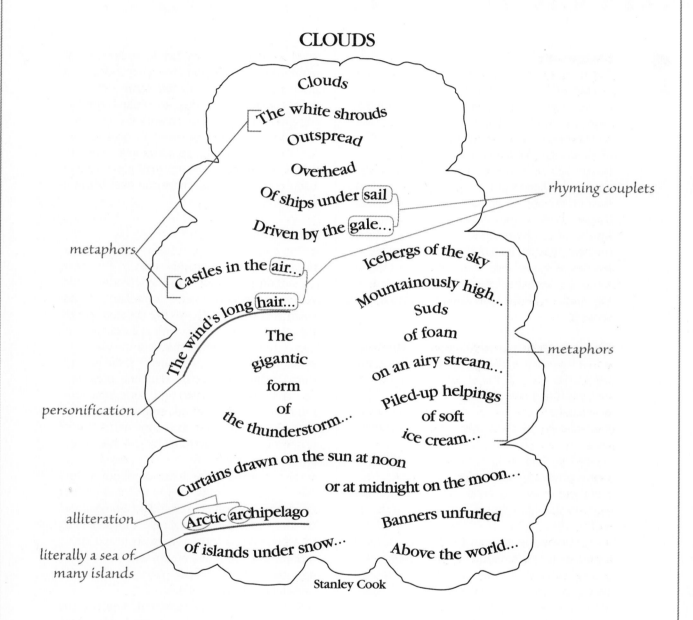

Clouds

The white shrouds

Outspread

Overhead

Of ships under sail

Driven by the gale...

Castles in the air...

The wind's long hair...

Icebergs of the sky

Mountainously high...

Suds

of foam

on an airy stream...

Piled-up helpings

of soft

ice cream...

The

gigantic

form

of

the thunderstorm...

Curtains drawn on the sun at noon

or at midnight on the moon...

Arctic archipelago

Banners unfurled

of islands under snow...

Above the world...

Stanley Cook

rhyming couplets

metaphors

metaphors

personification

alliteration

literally a sea of many islands

3: 1: T8: to express their views about a story or poem, identifying specific words and phrases to support their viewpoint

3: 1: T13: to collect suitable words and phrases, in order to write poems and short descriptions; design simple patterns with words, use repetitive phrases; write imaginative comparisons

3: 1: T14: to invent calligrams and a range of shape poems, selecting appropriate words and careful presentation. Build up class collections

Sir Gawain and the Green Knight

by Steve Barlow &
Steve Skidmore

Background

This is a play about putting on a play – a long-established device used by such playwrights as Shakespeare (for example, *A Midsummer Night's Dream*). All the actors in the play take on the roles of two characters, firstly a member of the drama group and secondly a character in the group's play. The setting is a school stage where Ms Clarke's drama group are rehearsing their production of Sir Gawaine and the Green Knight – a story from the times of King Arthur. Ms Clarke is determined to impress Mrs Phillips, the head teacher, who doesn't really approve of the drama group. The rehearsals are not going too well! This extract starts the play off. Ensure the reading of the playscript brings out the sense of fun and humour.

Shared reading and discussing the text

● Read the first exchange between Barry and Ms Clarke and ask the children what kind of text this is and how they know.
● Ask pairs of children to speculate what would immediately precede Ms Clarke's opening lines.
● Ask the children to finish Barry's unfinished words offstage, *Please, Miss, can I go to the…* Point out how this adds to the humour, as nothing should be heard from offstage during a play.
● Encourage the children to identify the main features of the structure of a playscript, for example characters' names on the left, spoken words on the right without speech marks, stage directions in brackets and italic, and the play divided into scenes and so on.
● Ask the children to look at the punctuation in the extract. Look in particular at commas and exclamation marks. Read Ms Clarke's words as she shouts at Barry (*Barry! Stop that!…*) with and without the punctuation to demonstrate its importance.
● Discuss the use of special language in drama, for example *take it away* meaning 'start the production' and *cue*, which is the signal given by the last words of one actor's speech for

another actor to enter, speak or perform an action. Ask the children for other words that belong to drama, for example *scene*.
● Encourage the children to discuss whether this performance of the drama production is likely to be a good one and to give reasons for their evaluation, for example that the actors aren't ready, King Arthur's crown is badly repaired, the audience can hear offstage comments.

Activities

● Drawing on the discussion about drama-related vocabulary, provide a list of the terms for writing and performing plays. (For example, *setting*, *dialogue*, *stage direction*, *props*, *characters*, *rehearsal*.) Ask the children to turn the list into a glossary by writing a definition by each term. Add to this list during the week.
● Put the children into groups of three and ask them to take turns in reading the playscript: one child to read setting and stage directions, the next to read Ms Clark and a third to read Barry. Encourage them to change parts. One or two groups could perform for the class using appropriate intonation.
● Have a whole-class discussion about a story the children all know well with three or four characters, for example *Little Red Riding Hood*. Use this information to model the beginning of a play of the chosen story. In mixed-ability groups, ask the children to write one small episode from the story in playscript form with one child acting as scribe.
● Chose a child to represent one of the characters in the play, for example Ms Clarke and put them in the 'hot-seat'. The rest of the class then ask questions, which have to be answered in role.

Extension/further reading

Watch a performance of a play at a theatre or invite a theatre group to perform in school. Alternatively, watch a video of a play being performed. Arrange a visit to a local theatre for a backstage tour.

3: 1: S2: to take account of the grammar and punctuation, e.g. sentences, speech marks, exclamation marks and commas to mark pauses, when reading aloud

3: 1: S9: to notice and investigate a range of other devices for presenting texts, e.g. italicised print

Sir Gawain and the Green Knight

setting the scene

Scene 1
The school stage is set as a chamber in King Arthur's castle. If you have a curtain, it should be closed at the beginning.

Ms Clarke: (*Offstage*) Well, I can't help it if King Arthur's crown is coming apart. Use some sticky tape or something.

Barry: (*Offstage*) Please, Miss, can I go to the...

Ms Clarke: (*Offstage*) No, you can't. I'm sorry but we're just about to start. You should have gone before.

(Ms Clarke comes to the front of the stage, looking flustered. She speaks to the audience where Mrs Phillips is supposedly sitting.)

Ms Clarke: Oh, Mrs Phillips, I'm so glad you could come to our final dress rehearsal. I know the Drama Group has been in a bit of hot water lately, what with the angels fighting the shepherds during the Nativity play, but we've all worked really hard this time.

(There is a loud crash offstage. Ms Clarke turns round.)

Ms Clarke: (*Shouting*) Barry! Stop that! Put the sword down!

Barry: (*Offstage*) Sorry, Miss.

Ms Clarke: (*Talking to Mrs Phillips*) Er, sorry about that. I'll just introduce the play and then we'll 'take it away', as they say.

(Ms Clarke coughs nervously.)

Ms Clarke: Good evening, ladies and gentlemen, and welcome to our Drama Group's presentation of the story of 'Sir Gawain and the Green Knight'. (*She waits. Nothing happens.*)

Ms Clarke: (*Whispers loudly*) Jason – that's your cue.

(The play begins. The curtain jerks open. The actors aren't ready and have to scamper to their places. King Arthur's crown has been stuck together in a hurry and not very well.)

characters with easily recognisable roles (pupil/ teacher)

commas to mark pauses between clauses

exclamation marks emphasise forcefulness

playscript conventions: character name, colon, line(s) of speech

stage directions written in italic

starts in the middle of the action

predictable missing word instantly establishes pupil role

example of comedy

informal speech versus formal speech as dress rehearsal begins

suspense

another comic effect (slapstick)

3: 1: T4: to read, prepare and present playscripts

3: 1: T5: to recognise the key differences between prose and playscript, e.g. by looking at dialogue, stage directions, layout of text in prose and playscripts

3: 1: T15: to write simple playscripts based on own reading and oral work

Odysseus and the Cyclops by Paul Copley

Background

This extract is from a play about Odysseus, the King of Ithaca, and a huge one-eyed giant Cyclops called Polyphemus. The story comes from a Greek myth which was told about 3000 years ago. This extract tells the story of how Odysseus outwitted the Cyclops. The story begins after the Trojan War, which lasted ten years and in which Odysseus had fought successfully. He and his friends, including Nik, Andreus and Alex, are sailing home but a violent storm forces them to land on an unknown island. They take shelter in a cave, taking with them a jug of wine. The Cyclops finds the men there when he returns with his sheep, and decides to eat some of them. Odysseus saves the rest of his companions by spearing the Cyclops in his one eye and blinding him. The survivors then escape by holding onto the undersides of sheep so Cyclops couldn't feel them with his hands.

Shared reading and discussing the text

● Read or tell the story of Odysseus from Term 2 (see page 44).

● Explain that this play is set on an unnamed island as Odysseus travels home after the Trojan War. Odysseus and his friends take shelter in the cave. In this extract, the friends are describing the huge and terrible Cyclops before the audience have an opportunity to see him, which heightens the expectation of terror. Refer to the story read or told earlier to explain how as the leader of the group of friends Odysseus is portrayed as brave, wise and full of ideas for their escape.

● Conceal with Post-it Notes the three stage directions that indicate how certain lines of speech are to be read (*In a terrified voice, In a booming voice, In a whisper*) and read the script through with the children, having allocated roles to pairs. Play the narrator yourself.

● Ask the children to speculate on the concealed stage directions. You could ask them how they think each character might be feeling. Reveal the directions.

● Ask the children to find key words and phrases that describe the Cyclops, and discuss how the group of friends inside the cave might feel hearing and then seeing this fearsome giant approaching. How are their feelings of fear built up?

● Ask the children to predict how the scene might develop with Odysseus having the ideas that allow most of his friends and lastly himself to escape from the giant.

● Discuss the layout of the play including the role of the narrator and the use of stage directions in brackets to tell the actors how to speak the lines.

Activities

● The children can work on developing expressive reading of the extract in guided or independent groups. Prompt them to use appropriate voices and to use the punctuation as a guide to how the lines should be read. After one reading, they could swap roles.

● Ask the children to write the next part of the play where the Cyclops, Polyphemus, discovers the Greek men in the cave and decides to gobble down two of the friends, spitting out their belts and sandals. This could be done individually or in pairs.

● Ask the children to draw annotated pictures of their own idea of the one-eyed Cyclops.

● Ask the children what Odysseus' escape plan might be and model writing the beginning of this in shared writing.

Extension/further reading

Read a different Greek (or Roman) myth and turn the story into a play. See for example, *The Orchard Book of Greek Gods and Goddesses* and *The Orchard Book of Roman Myths*.

Encourage the children to talk about times they have been terrified of a real or imagined event. Ask them to write an outline for a story about it and then develop a short playscript for part or all of the story. Alternatively take a frightening episode from a book, for example a *Harry Potter* story, for the children to work on.

3: 1: S2: to take account of the grammar and punctuation, e.g. sentences, speech marks, exclamation marks and commas to mark pauses, when reading aloud

3: 1: S6: to secure knowledge of question marks and exclamation marks in reading, understand their purpose and use appropriately in own writing

3: 1: T3: to be aware of the different voices in stories using dramatised readings, showing differences between the narrator and different characters used

Odysseus and the Cyclops

setting the scene

Scene 3   Inside the cave

Narrator   *Night fell before they had finished eating. The cave was a very gloomy place. The only light was coming from the glowing embers of the fire in the middle of the floor. Nik and Andreas kept watch at the doorway. Suddenly the ground began to tremble and shake. They could hear boulders crunching and stones crashing down the cliffs into the sea below.*

narrator's speech also italicised to stand out from other characters

italicised stage directions

stage directions indicate how line is to be spoken

Alex   *(In a terrified voice)* It's an earthquake!

Odysseus   It sounds more like the footsteps of a giant.

Nik   Look out, look out!

Andreas   There *is* a giant coming.

Nik   He's as big as twenty men.

Alex   That's big!

Andreas   He's so big that he's using a tree for a walking stick.

Alex   That's really big.

Nik   His face is hairy and dirty and as big as the moon.

Andreas   His teeth are like mouldy tree stumps.

Nik   And he's only got one eye.

Odysseus   Only one eye?

Nik   One massive round eye in the middle of his huge dirty forehead.

Narrator   *At that moment they all heard the great rumbling voice of Polyphemus the Cyclops. The ground shook as he spoke to his sheep and goats.*

Polyphemus   *(In a booming voice)* Here we are my beauties! Home at last! I'm ready for my supper now. I'm sure I could eat a dozen men and still not be full!

Nik   Hear that? What are we going to do, Odysseus?

Odysseus   Ssh! Quietly now. We must run and hide at the back of the cave. Quick!

Narrator   *As Odysseus and his friends watched from the shadows, the huge and terrible Cyclops milked all his goats and his sheep. Then he pulled a great lump of stone across the doorway of the cave. Odysseus whispered to his friends...*

Odysseus   *(In a whisper)* Now we are trapped. Even if we could get past the giant it would take more than twenty men to move that stone.

friends of Odysseus

question mark to indicate curiosity and surprise; note effect on intonation

contrasting voices in text

build-up of suspense created by similes

different effects created by exclamation marks: one to denote surprise, the other urgency

a double bind!

3: 1: T4: to read, prepare and present playscripts

3: 1: T5: to recognise the key differences between prose and playscript, e.g. by looking at dialogue, stage directions, layout of text in prose and playscripts

3: 1: T15: to write simple playscripts based on own reading and oral work

The Curse of the Baskervilles

Background

This extract has as its main characters two of the most famous detectives created in fiction, Sherlock Holmes and his assistant Dr Watson. Sir Arthur Conan Doyle created these two characters in 1887, and in 1902 he wrote the novel *The Hound of the Baskervilles* on which this play is based. It is the story about the legend of a giant hound which is said to haunt the Baskerville family and their home Baskerville Hall. In this extract the legend now appears to be threatening the new owner of the house, Henrietta Baskerville (in the original novel a Henry Baskerville is the owner of the house). Holmes and Watson do, of course, save Henrietta's life by brilliant detective work. They discover that the legend of the ghostly hound is being used in a murder attempt by Mr Stapleton who was hoping to inherit the Hall.

In this extract, Henrietta comes to ask Sherlock and Watson for their help about a threatening letter she has received.

Shared reading and discussing the text

● Explain that this extract is based on a book written over 100 years ago, a mystery story with two characters – Sherlock Holmes and his assistant – who have become two of the most famous detectives ever created in fiction. They were famous for being able to solve a crime with very few clues. Holmes would sometimes use the catchphrase *'Elementary, my dear Watson'* to 'modestly' explain his genius.
● Building on their work done with 'Sir Gawain and the Green Knight' (page 28) and 'Odysseus and the Cyclops' (page 30), ask the children to discuss in pairs all the distinguishing features of the playscript.
● Split the class into four and read the extract together, with each group taking one part.

● Finally, conclude the story for the children by telling them that Henrietta is saved from a horrendous death when Holmes and Watson discover that Mr Stapleton, a neighbour, has devised an evil plan to have Henrietta killed and inherit Baskerville Hall himself.

Activities

● The children can work on their reading of the script in guided or independent reading.
● Ask the children to highlight examples of punctuation in the playscript, such as commas to indicate pauses and question and exclamation marks. Ask them what the effect would be on reading the playscript aloud if this punctuation were not there.
● Ask the children to write their own playscripts for one of these scenarios:
   – Henrietta leaves the room and tells a friend about her visit to Holmes and Watson.
   – The discussion Holmes and Watson have after Henrietta leaves the room.
● Explain to the children that the other scenes of the play take place at Baskerville Hall in the middle of Dartmoor, which can be a very eerie place when the mists descend. Ask the children to imagine the next scene of the play when Holmes and Watson arrive at Baskerville Hall, and to describe it in the most frightening way possible. Build up a class list of suitable words and phrases, for example *swirling mist, howling wind, haunted rooms*, and so on.

Extension/further reading

Ask the children to collect information on other fictional detectives from literature and television.

Abridged versions of stories about Sherlock Holmes include *Sherlock Holmes in 'The Hound of the Baskervilles'* (Picture Lions).

3: 1: S2: to take account of the grammar and punctuation, e.g. sentences, speech marks, exclamation marks and commas to mark pauses, when reading aloud

3: 1: S6: to secure knowledge of question marks and exclamation marks in reading, understand their purpose and use appropriately in own writing

3: 1: T3: to be aware of the different voices in stories using dramatised readings, showing differences between the narrator and different characters used

economic description of setting (in comparison with prose)

The Curse of the Baskervilles

Scene 1   Inside Sherlock Holmes' flat

question mark indicates question that's not apparent from words alone (ellipsis for 'Are you Mr Holmes?')

Narrator	Sherlock Holmes, the famous detective, lives in London. He and Dr Watson, his assistant, are having breakfast in their flat in Baker Street. There is a knock at the door and Henrietta Baskerville enters.
Henrietta	Mr Holmes? I need help. I have just arrived from America and found this letter waiting for me at my hotel.
Holmes	Read it out, Watson.
Dr Watson	'If you value your life, stay away from Baskerville Hall.' What does it mean?
Henrietta	My uncle has just died. I didn't even know him but he has left me his house, Baskerville Hall. It's a great big old house in Devon.
Holmes	How did your uncle die?
Henrietta	He'd gone into the garden last thing at night and when he didn't return, the housekeeper went to look for him. She found him lying dead on the path.
Dr Watson	Did he have a heart attack?
Henrietta	Not exactly. That's what makes it so spooky. His face was a mask of terror. It looked as though he had died of fear!
Holmes	Baskerville Hall is in the middle of Dartmoor.
Watson	It must be close to Dartmoor prison.
Holmes	Ah, a prisoner escaped from Dartmoor prison yesterday. Perhaps that is connected with the letter in some way.

contrast apostrophe 's' for possession with apostrophe for contraction

questions and answers used to move the story along

comma used to indicate pause when reading

build-up of fear; atmospheric words and phrases

device often used in plays: reading a letter out loud, as all information has to be conveyed through dialogue

note possibilities of inference – was it a natural death?

exclamation mark to denote horror

remote marshy land in Devon

connotations for reader of fear evoked by moor and prison

3: 1: T4: to read, prepare and present playscripts

3: 1: T5: to recognise the key differences between prose and playscript, e.g. by looking at dialogue, stage directions, layout of text in prose and playscripts

3: 1: T15: to write simple playscripts based on own reading and oral work

Wes Magee

Background

This biographical piece about the poet and writer, Wes Magee, is the first of four non-fiction texts. Organised into several clear sections, the piece moves from the opening description of where he lives to some brief, chronologically ordered details about how he began writing. The piece then slips into report mode again as the reader learns about Magee's working routine and the rewards he gains from his work. One of his poems, 'Football Dreaming', is also provided, as well as a bibliography.

Shared reading and discussing the text

● Read the text through with the children and ask them why they think it was written and where they might expect to find it (for example, in a book on poets, on a poster about the poet and so on). Ask the children if it is fiction or non-fiction, explaining the terms if necessary.

● Can they work out what a bibliography is?

● Divide the class into four and ask each quarter – working in pairs – to choose the key word, phrase or sentence from one of the four main paragraphs. Use the children's suggestions to devise sub-headings for each paragraph and ask the children how these would need to be written so they stand out (for example, using a different font, capitals or italic).

Activities

● Discuss what else the children would like to know about Wes Magee. Ask them to write suitable questions, for example *Are you writing a book at present?*

● Ask the children to write down some questions to ask other children in order to find out about their lives, for example *Where were you born? What hobbies do you have? What is the name of your favourite book?* Try them out.

● Working in pairs, the children could write biographical paragraphs about each other, after agreeing what each paragraph should be about, for example where they were born and where they live now; their family and pets; their school; hobbies or favourite activities. In mixed-ability pairs, the most able writer could act as scribe.

● The children could develop this work by presenting their information about their partners using ICT in a similar style to the text about Wes Magee. This could include a favourite poem or a poem the child has written, as well as a drawing or photograph of the child with appropriate captions. Encourage the children to use a range of devices including enlarged and italicised print, different fonts, headings and boxed text.

Extension/further reading

The children could research another children's author using reference books and the Internet and present information about their chosen subject as a biographical text. Discuss what other information the class would like to know about the author.

Wes Magee has written a number of poetry collections and compiled poetry anthologies, some of which are detailed in the bibliography part of the text.

3: 1: S9: to notice and investigate a range of other devices for presenting texts, e.g. speech bubbles, enlarged or italicised print, captions and headings, inset text

3: 1: T17: to understand the distinction between fact and fiction; to use terms 'fact', 'fiction' and 'non-fiction' appropriately

3: 1: T18: to notice differences in the style and structure of fiction and non-fiction writing

present tense, typical of information texts

heading in bold, stands out

general introduction

an example of a poem written by Wes Magee

what he believes in present tense

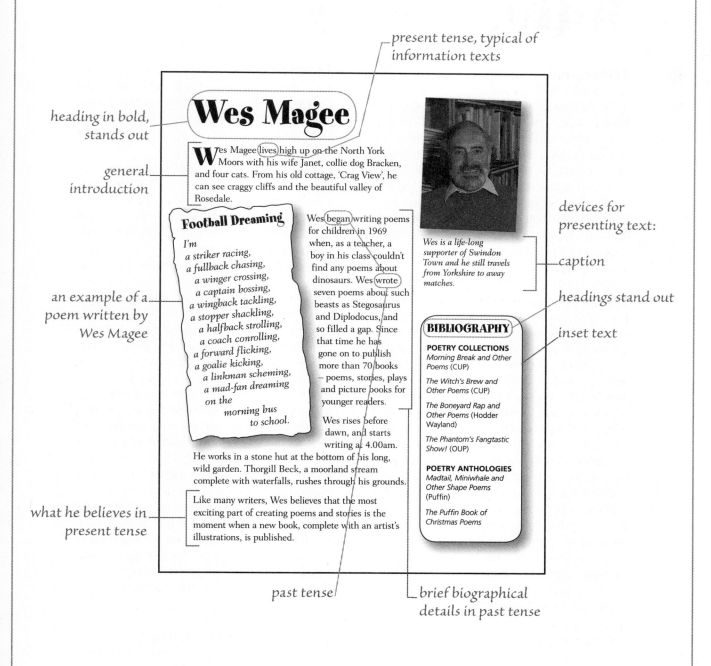

Wes Magee

Wes Magee lives high up on the North York Moors with his wife Janet, collie dog Bracken, and four cats. From his old cottage, 'Crag View', he can see craggy cliffs and the beautiful valley of Rosedale.

Football Dreaming

I'm
a striker racing,
a fullback chasing,
  a winger crossing,
   a captain bossing,
  a wingback tackling,
 a stopper shackling,
  a halfback strolling,
   a coach conrolling,
  a forward flicking,
 a goalie kicking,
  a linkman scheming,
   a mad-fan dreaming
     on the
        morning bus
          to school.

Wes began writing poems for children in 1969 when, as a teacher, a boy in his class couldn't find any poems about dinosaurs. Wes wrote seven poems about such beasts as Stegosaurus and Diplodocus, and so filled a gap. Since that time he has gone on to publish more than 70 books – poems, stories, plays and picture books for younger readers.

Wes rises before dawn, and starts writing at 4.00am. He works in a stone hut at the bottom of his long, wild garden. Thorgill Beck, a moorland stream complete with waterfalls, rushes through his grounds.

Like many writers, Wes believes that the most exciting part of creating poems and stories is the moment when a new book, complete with an artist's illustrations, is published.

Wes is a life-long supporter of Swindon Town and he still travels from Yorkshire to away matches.

BIBLIOGRAPHY

POETRY COLLECTIONS
Morning Break and Other Poems (CUP)

The Witch's Brew and Other Poems (CUP)

The Boneyard Rap and Other Poems (Hodder Wayland)

The Phantom's Fangtastic Show! (OUP)

POETRY ANTHOLOGIES
Madtail, Miniwhale and Other Shape Poems (Puffin)

The Puffin Book of Christmas Poems

devices for presenting text:

caption

headings stand out

inset text

past tense

brief biographical details in past tense

3: 1: T19: to locate information, using contents, index, headings, sub-headings, page nos., bibliographies

3: 1: T21: to read information passages, and identify main points or gist of text, e.g. by noting or underlining key words or phrases, listing the 4 or 5 key points covered

Telling the time

Background

This extract demonstrates a range of devices used to organise information in non-fiction texts, such as headings, bold print and a variety of fonts. It also demonstrates how text can be supported with images. The extract also contains specialised language, which will require the children to develop their skills in using and making dictionaries and glossaries. The informal tone and style of the italicised introductory paragraph stands in marked contrast to the rest of the piece.

Shared reading and discussing the text

● Ask the children which section of the library they think this book comes from (for example, the science section). Remind the children of the Wes Magee extract and ask them whether they think 'Telling the time' is fiction or non-fiction. What reasons can they give?

● Read the three sections separately and discuss the gist of each to demonstrate that the information has been organised into clear areas. The first section introduces the topic, the second section looks at the reason for the development of units of time and the third looks at the development of clocks. Can the children spot the lead sentence for each?

● Ask the children to identify unfamiliar words and explain that this non-fiction text contains language that is special to the subject, for example *clepsydra*. Explain that the word *sundial* is presented in bold print because the word appears in the book's glossary.

● Ask the children why the image of the sundial is there (to make the text clearer and add a visual dimension to the page). What do they notice about the caption for the image? Why has the publisher used different fonts, bold print and enlarged headings? Ask the children to start a collection of different fonts and headings from newspapers and magazines.

Activities

● As shared writing, make a list with the children of all the different presentational devices they discussed above. Write a code by each one:

– main heading	MH
– sub-heading	SH
– font size	FS
– font type	FT

and so on. Working in groups with their own copies of the text, the children can then go on to label all these features.

● Ask the children which of the two main sections they found most interesting and then put the children into pairs who have chosen the same section. Explain that they and their partners should write down the most important facts in their chosen section. Then ask the children to add any more information they may already know.

● Ask the children to record all the occasions when they need to know the time accurately during their week, for example for the start of school, television programmes and football matches, to catch buses, trains, and so on. Provide them with the title 'Why time is important to me' and ask them to write a general introductory statement, followed by a bulleted list.

● Tell the children to build up a word bank of any new vocabulary from the text, for example *sundial*, *clepsydra*. They could add other words from other books they have read about time, to build up a glossary.

Extension/further reading

There are several good books about time, including *What's the Big Idea? Time and the Universe* by John Gribbin (Hodder Children's Books) and *Nuffield Science and Literacy Big Book 2: Time and Space* by Derek Bell (Collins Educational).

3: 1: W13: to collect new words from reading and work in other subjects and create ways of categorising and logging them, e.g. personal dictionaries, glossaries

3: 1: S9: to notice and investigate a range of other devices for presenting texts, e.g. speech bubbles, enlarged or italicised print, captions and headings, inset text. Explore purposes and collect examples

direct question and address to reader

informal tone

heading; enlarged font size

general introductory paragraph in italic

sub-heading in smaller font

sub-heading explains main point of section

caption provides detail about image

1st person – inclusive tone drawing reader in

3rd person

past tense verbs

sub-heading indicates this section is about history of clocks (play on words!)

bold print indicates this word appears in the book's glossary

specialised language

main point of section

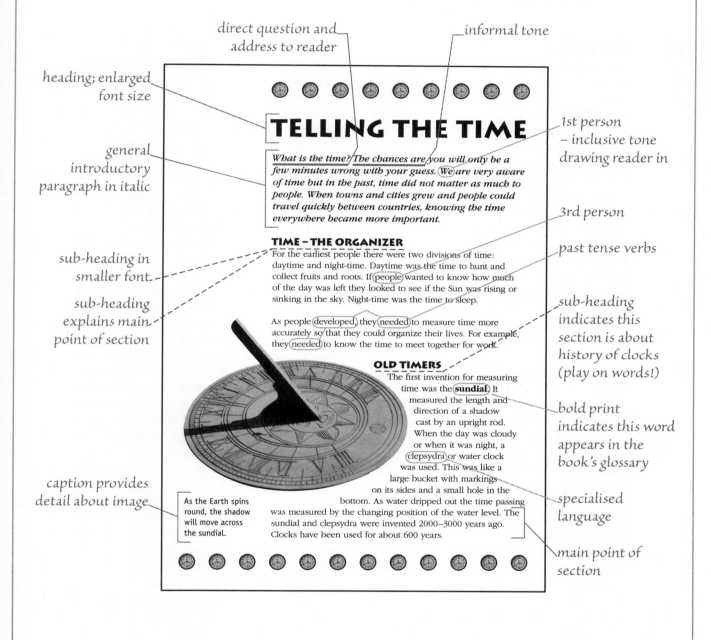

TELLING THE TIME

What is the time? The chances are you will only be a few minutes wrong with your guess. We are very aware of time but in the past, time did not matter as much to people. When towns and cities grew and people could travel quickly between countries, knowing the time everywhere became more important.

TIME – THE ORGANIZER

For the earliest people there were two divisions of time: daytime and night-time. Daytime was the time to hunt and collect fruits and roots. If people wanted to know how much of the day was left they looked to see if the Sun was rising or sinking in the sky. Night-time was the time to sleep.

As people developed, they needed to measure time more accurately so that they could organize their lives. For example, they needed to know the time to meet together for work.

OLD TIMERS

The first invention for measuring time was the **sundial**. It measured the length and direction of a shadow cast by an upright rod. When the day was cloudy or when it was night, a clepsydra or water clock was used. This was like a large bucket with markings on its sides and a small hole in the bottom. As water dripped out the time passing was measured by the changing position of the water level. The sundial and clepsydra were invented 2000–3000 years ago. Clocks have been used for about 600 years.

As the Earth spins round, the shadow will move across the sundial.

3: 1: T17: to understand the distinction between fact and fiction; to use terms 'fact', 'fiction' and 'non-fiction' appropriately

3: 1: T18: to notice differences in the style and structure of fiction and non-fiction writing

How did the Vikings live?

Background

Reports describe how things are, or were. They usually start with a general opening statement. The following paragraphs are then organised into areas of related interest. This structure is often reflected in the layout, with the use of headings, sub-headings and illustrations. As this is a historical report, the past tense is used.

This extract gives information about the Vikings, who were Scandinavian farmers and fishermen until about the 8th century, when their amazing skill at building boats allowed them to travel vast distances. The Vikings became great explorers, traders, violent raiders and finally settlers in the empire they established across the British Isles and south-west France. This extract describes Viking farms and towns – in particular, Jorvik.

Shared reading and discussing the text

● Ask the children if they can tell, just by looking at the piece, whether it is fiction or non-fiction. Can they give their reasons? Use this to elicit their understanding about the presentational devices explored in the previous text on time (for example, sub-headings).
● Find the word *archaeologists* towards the end of the extract and ask if anyone knows what it means and why it might be an important word in a text about people who lived long ago. Tell the children that we know about the Vikings from archaeological finds. We also know about them because of written accounts from the time. For instance, a monk in Northumberland wrote this about a Viking raid – *...they came like stinging hornets to Britain... like ravening wolves, plundering, devouring, slaughtering.*
● Before reading the text, ask the children what information they can glean from the photograph. Now read the text through with them.
● Look at the first two paragraphs under 'Viking town life'. Point out how this introduces a change of subject from farming and gives some background information on Jorvik.

● Point out that the text tells us two types of information: how the Vikings lived and how we know this.

Activities

● Model underlining the key words in the very first paragraph of the text. Demonstrate how this helps to identify the main point of the paragraph, for example *The Vikings became settlers in the Orkney and Shetland Islands.* Tell the children to work in pairs and identify the main point of the rest of the paragraphs by underlining key words and then recording these as a sentence or two. Select several pairs of children to read their main points to the class. For example, *Vikings also settled in a town they called Jorvik. Parts of the town have been preserved because of the wet ground. It was a busy place with many houses.*
● Ask the children to make a glossary of new and specialised words from the text, for example *settler, raider, byre, threshing, bathhouse.* Prompt them to infer the meaning from the context, then arrange the words in alphabetical order. Discuss their suggestions for definitions.
● Using a range of books on Vikings, ask the children in pairs to research another area, for example Viking ships or religious beliefs. Ask them to record the main points in each paragraph. The information could then be presented to the class.

Extension/further reading

Provide a map of Europe and point out the places mentioned in the text – Norway, Orkney and Shetland Islands, and York.

Use the children's understanding about the Vikings and what they have learnt from the text as the basis for a story writing activity. They could write about a child living in Jorvik.

There are a large number of excellent books about the Vikings, including *Vikings, Invaders and Settlers* by Tony Trigg (Wayland) and *Horrible Histories: The Vicious Vikings* by Terry Deary (Scholastic Hippo).

main heading made into a question

islands off north-east coast of Scotland within sailing distance of Norway

sub-heading

to save cutting and carrying more stone

a cowshed

to beat out grain from husks

a communal building where people could take baths – there were no bathrooms in houses

linking paragraph – takes reader from description of farms to description of Jorvik

photograph helps explain text and makes subject more 'alive'

evidence

introduction of main subject of section

photograph caption in italic

past tense verbs

evidence

people who study objects and remains from the past

use of dates and numbers typical of factual report

HOW DID THE
VIKINGS LIVE?

The Orkney and Shetland Islands suited the Vikings. The landscape, the weather, the harsh life of these northern islands were like those at home in Norway. They were settlers here, not raiders.

The Viking farmer's life
Viking farms were often built on the ruins of earlier buildings, perhaps re-using the stone. They built farmhouses with low stone walls. A farm would have a 'hall house' for living in, often oblong-shaped. Then there would be separate outbuildings: a byre (for cattle), a stable, a barn for threshing and storing corn, and perhaps a bathhouse.

▲ *These are the ruins of a 9th-century Viking farm – part of the Jarlshof settlement on Shetland.*

Viking town life
But many Vikings lived further south, inland amongst the English, and in towns. Their lives were different from those of the Orkney farmers.

When the Vikings captured Eoforwic (York) in 866, it must have seemed a disaster to the English residents. But over the next thirty years the Vikings who came and settled there built a defensive wall, new streets, and another bridge. They called the 'Vikingized' town Jorvik.

We know many things about Jorvik, because the wet ground has preserved parts of the town. Near the Rivers Ouse and Foss in Jorvik many things that would normally decay have been preserved by the damp conditions.

Viking Jorvik was a very busy place, crammed with people. New thatched timber houses were built for the newcomers. To get more people in, the houses were set sideways to the streets.

Behind the houses, stretching down towards the river, were workshops, then rubbish pits and wells, and warehouses. Archaeologists have worked out that by 1066 (when the Normans came) York had about 10,000 people living in nearly 2,000 houses.

A new lemur discovered

Background

This extract comes from the book *Wildlife in the News* by John Craven and Mark Carwardine in which they report on conservation stories that have made the news. They examine the problems being faced by some of the threatened wildlife and habitats around the world and look at the tremendous efforts which are being made to save them. In this extract, the information is organised into paragraphs each with its own clearly defined key idea, and this makes it a good example of the way reports are often constructed.

Shared reading and discussing the text

● Tell the children that this is an extract from a book that focuses on conservation stories that have been reported in the media.

● Read the extract with the children and ask them to pick out words that are specific to the subject of the report, for example *species*, *endangered*, *rare* and *loggers*. Discuss the meanings of the words with the children, encouraging them to predict their meanings from the context.

● Explain to the children that this is a report. Working in twos or threes, can they work out what the purpose of a report might be?

● Re-read as necessary and ask the children what the difference is between the first and subsequent paragraphs. Do they notice that the first paragraph serves as a general introductory statement and the following information is organised into paragraphs that focus on one area of information at a time? Look at the subsequent paragraphs separately and identify the main points in each.

● Ask what the photograph adds – if anything – to their understanding of the report. Are there any other visuals that could have been used here (for example, a map)?

● Discuss how the extract has two types of information: the history of the discovery of the lemur (in the past tense) and a description of the lemur (in the present tense).

Activities

● In shared writing, select an animal familiar to the children and ask them to contribute information, which you record on the board. Discuss how the information could be organised into paragraphs and write the paragraph headings, for example a general opening statement, what the animal looks like, what it eats, where it lives, and so on.

● Tell the children to use these paragraph headings to organise the information into the appropriate paragraphs. Ask several children to discuss what information they have written in each paragraph.

● Provide a range of information books on animals. Tell the children to select a book with a partner and decide which animal they are going to research. Some pairs of children could be given different books so they have to draw information from more than one source. Write down the four headings for them to research (explaining and modelling this if necessary). These can be the ones used earlier. Tell the children to skim the book to find information and then write the main facts under the correct paragraph heading.

● Explain to the children that they are going to plan and design a poster that will give information about the lemur, for example why it is at risk and how it can be saved. In groups, ask the children to decide what information they think should be included and how to present this information clearly.

Extension/further reading

The DFEE (2000) publication *The National Literacy Strategy: Grammar for Writing* contains an exercise on organising information into paragraphs (see Unit 9, pages 50–1).

Using an atlas, locate Madagascar and the town of Ranomafana. Children could also use a CD-ROM encyclopaedia and links to the Internet to look up further information about the lemur and the rainforest environment in which it lives.

general introductory 1st paragraph about how the lemur was discovered

a group of animals sharing common characteristics

subsequent paragraphs focus on one area of information at a time:

2nd paragraph: what it looks like (moves into report mode describing lemurs)

3rd paragraph: information about other species of lemur

4th paragraph: destruction of the lemur's habitat and why the discovery of the new species of lemur may help

5th paragraph: how more varieties of lemur are being discovered by scientists

A NEW LEMUR

D I S C O V E R E D

1 n 1986 an exciting discovery was made in Madagascar. A new species of lemur was found in a small area of rainforest near the town of Ranomafana, in the south-east of the country. It has been named the golden bamboo lemur.

2 The new species looks rather like a monkey, to which it is distantly related. Roughly a metre in length, half of which consists of a black-tipped tail, it has small round ears, golden eyebrows, orange cheeks and a rich reddish-brown coat. Two individuals of the new species, a male and a female, have been captured by scientists in Madagascar. They are now in captivity in the zoo at Antananarivo, the capital city, where they are being studied closely.

3 There are two other species of bamboo lemur living in the Ranomafana area: the grey gentle lemur, which is quite common in Madagascar, and the greater bamboo lemur, which is so rare that it was believed to be extinct until its rediscovery in 1972.

4 In recent years, large areas of the forest have been chopped down by loggers and by local farmers for land crops, so the lemurs and all the other animals living there are at risk. However, the discovery of the golden bamboo lemur may have saved the day. It has encouraged the Government of Madagascar to consider establishing the forest as a national park. With immediate intervention of this kind, Ranomafana and all its wildlife could still be saved.

5 As scientists explore new areas of rainforest in Madagascar, more lemur species are likely to be identified. The latest discovery is the golden-crowned sifaka, which has a shock of golden orange on the crown of its head. There are only a few hundred of these beautiful animals left, making them one of the most endangered of all the lemurs.

past tense for reporting events in the past: the discovery of the lemur

changes to present tense for description of the lemur

no longer in existence

lumberjacks – people who cut down trees

under threat

King Midas

by Geraldine McCaughrean

Background

This Greek myth was first told 3000 years ago. Myths were a way for the Ancient Greeks to make sense of the world, and explain things they did not understand. Usually about gods, heroes and, in the case of this extract, foolish mortals, they also deal with themes such as good and evil, folly and wisdom and other concerns of human nature. The stories came from the oral tradition and much later they were written down with children in mind. This story about King Midas is not about the heroic deeds of a god, but of a rather stupid and greedy man who wishes that everything he touches would turn to gold. It is a story with its own moral and many of the elements of traditional stories, such as the granting of a wish and objects being turned to gold.

Shared reading and discussing the text

● Tell the children that they are going to read a story that was first told 3000 years ago. Read this first sentence of the story: *There once was a king called Midas who was almost as stupid as he was greedy.* Explain that King Midas was asked to judge a music competition between two gods – Pan and Apollo. Midas let Pan win as he was his friend. Apollo was so angry that he punished Midas by giving him long donkey's ears. Midas kept these hidden under a tall hat. The story continues with this extract.

● Read up to *and bit into it*. What do the children think will happen next? Will the King be made happy by his wish that everything he touches is turned into gold?

● Read the rest of the extract. How do the children think King Midas felt as his son was turned to gold? Can the children suggest what the theme of the story is? (Greed, foolishness.)

● Can the children pick out the mythical elements of the story, for example a character with supernatural powers?

● Read the extract again and ask the children to discuss possible ways of how the story ends, then share their ideas with the class.

● Ask the children to tell you what kind of person they think King Midas is and to give reasons for their opinions. For example, he is unpleasant (he throws a stone at the satyr); he is greedy (he asks for everything he touches to be turned into gold). Do they think Midas will learn anything from what happened in the story and, if so, what do they think this lesson is? As a class, make a list of adjectives to describe the king for the children to use in their writing.

● The grant of a wish is a common element of traditional stories (and for the wish to cause trouble rather than happiness). Do the children know of other stories that use this theme?

Activities

● Ask the children to imagine that they are King Midas and write the story from his point of view in the first person. Focus on how his feelings change as the story progresses, such as from greedy to remorseful. They can include what they think he might have learnt from his experience. With lower-ability groups in guided writing, brainstorm King Midas' feelings.

● In shared writing, plan and model writing a possible ending for this story based on some of the suggestions the children made earlier. For example, focus on how Midas felt/the return of the satyr/the removal of wish/the lesson learnt! When the children have decided which ending they think is most suitable, ask them to complete the story in groups using the plan.

● Ask the children to imagine another character who could be granted a wish and write down what this would be. Ask them to use this as the title of a story. They will need to include information about this character, who will grant the wish and how the wish could change the character's life for better or worse.

Extension/further reading

The children could read the whole of the story of King Midas or another Greek myth. Geraldine McCaughrean has written a number of collections, including *The Orchard Book of Greek Myths,* from which this extract is taken, and *100 World Myths and Legends* (Orion).

3: 2: T2: to identify typical story themes, e.g. trials and forfeits, good over evil, weak over strong, wise over foolish

3: 2: T3 to identify and discuss main and recurring characters, evaluate their behaviour and justify views

3: 2: T8: to write portraits of characters, using story text to describe behaviour and characteristics, and presenting portraits in a variety of ways

indication that the story has already started

mixture of mythical and everyday elements

natural speech sounds

revealing of his character – childish, slightly ridiculous

dramatic moment – as with many wishes in literature, King Midas' wish has been granted exactly

alliteration

one-word sentence for effect

repetition heightens effect

to hide his ass's ears

typical feature of myths and traditional tales: a strange character with supernatural powers

human greed: traditional story theme

Midas does not listen to the warning

demonstrates his unpleasant character

onomatopoeia

the dash indicates the word is unfinished

tragic outcome

KING MIDAS

Meanwhile, Midas (wearing his tall cap, of course) was walking in his garden when he met a satyr—half-man, half-horse. The satyr was lost. Midas gave him breakfast and directed him on his way.

"I'm so grateful," said the satyr. "Permit me to reward you. I shall grant you one wish."

He could have wished to be rid of his ass's ears, but no. At once Midas' head filled with pictures of money, wealth, treasure... *gold*! His eyes glistened. "Oh please, please! Grant that everything I touch turns to gold!"

"Oof. Not a good idea," said the satyr. "Think again."

But Midas insisted. That was his wish. The satyr shrugged and went on his way.

"Huh! I knew it was too good to be true," said King Midas and he was so disappointed that he picked up a pebble to throw after the satyr.

The stone turned to gold in his palm.

"My wish! The satyr granted it after all!" cried Midas, and did a little dance on the spot. He ran to a tree and touched it. Sure enough, the twigs and branches turned to gold. He ran back to his palace and stroked every wall, chair, table and lamp. They all turned to gold. When he brushed against the curtains, even they turned solid with a sudden clang.

"Prepare me a feast!" Midas commanded. "Being rich makes me hungry!"

The servants ran to fetch meat and bread, fruit and wine, while Midas touched each dish and plate (because it pleased him to eat off gold). When the food arrived, he clutched up a wing of chicken and bit into it. Clang. It was hard and cold between his lips. The celery scratched his tongue. The bread broke a tooth. Every bite of food turned to gold as he touched it. The wine rattled in its goblet, solid as an egg in an egg cup.

"Don't stand there staring! Fetch me something I can eat!" Midas told a servant, giving him a push... But it was a golden statue of a servant that toppled over and fell with a thud.

Just then, the queen came in. "What's this I hear about a wish?" she asked, and went to kiss her husband.

"Don't come near! Don't touch me!" he shrieked, and jumped away from her. But his little son, who was too young to understand, ran and hugged Midas around the knees. "Papa! Papa! Pa—"

Silence. His son was silent. The boy's golden arms were still hooped round Midas' knees. His little golden mouth was open, but no sound came out.

3: 2: T9: to write a story plan for own myth, fable or traditional tale, using story theme from reading but substituting different characters or changing the setting

3: 2: T10: to write alternative sequels to traditional stories using same characters and settings, identifying typical phrases and expressions from story and using these to help structure the writing

Odysseus

by Geraldine McCaughrean

Extract 1

Background

This extract uses a story from the *Odyssey*, which, together with the *Iliad*, is believed to have been written by Homer. These are epic poems that were probably composed in the Greek settlements on the west coast of Asia Minor (Turkey) sometime in the 9th century BC. The *Odyssey* tells the epic story of Odysseus' ten-year journey home to Ithaca after the Trojan War. During the journey Odysseus has to face many dangers. In this extract Odysseus meets the Cyclops…

Shared reading and discussing the text

● Tell the children that this excerpt has been translated and retold from a Greek legend thought to have been written in about the 9th century BC. (Check that the children understand the BC system of numbering years and explain it if not.) Explain that the Greeks believed that the gods could meet ordinary people and so their stories mix gods and humans together. Tell them that this particular story comes from a book called the *Odyssey*, which tells the story of Odysseus' journey home to Ithaca and the many adventures he encounters after ten years fighting in the Trojan War. Tell the children that this journey is so famous that long wandering journeys of any kind are now often called odysseys.

● Remind the children of the work they did on Odysseus in Term 1 (see page 30). Tell them that they are going to revisit this tale, but in a different form.

● Read the text and discuss how the opening paragraph sets the scene for the story. Discuss how the repetition of *at last* makes it clear the war had lasted a long time.

● Tell the children that the one-eyed giant is called a Cyclops and discuss with them the paragraph that describes his appearance.

● Explain that Odysseus is the hero of the story and discuss with the children the qualities that they think a hero might be expected to have.

● Select children to read the opening paragraph of the story, after explaining why commas are important in adding meaning and demonstrating how sentences should be read.

● Remind the children what a compound word is, such as *playground*, and ask them to find examples of these words in the text.

Activities

● Tell the children to write a synopsis of the story so far. Give them key words such as *war, Odysseus, island* and *cave* to support their writing.

● Ask the children to predict what they think might happen next in the story. How do they think the hero Odysseus and his men will escape from the Cyclops? Working in pairs, ask them to plan the next part of the story, after discussing different methods of planning and demonstrating one of these methods. Share some of the children's plans with the class.

● Ask the children to return to the plan made for the continuation of the story and use the plan to write the next part of the story.

● Remind the children of what they read about the Cyclops and tell them to use this information to write their own description of the mythical creature. Then ask them to draw their impression of him and label it.

● Return to the list of compound words found in the text and ask the children to add to the list with words they know. Let them use a dictionary to add further to this list.

Extension/further reading

Ask the children to imagine a mythical creature of their own. Encourage them to write about the features of their creature in as much detail as possible and then give this information to a partner. Their partner then draws the creature, using the written description, and the pair should discuss how accurate they think the drawing is.

Look at *Greek Myths for Young Children* by Marcia Williams (Walker Books) and *Greek Myths and Legends* by C Evans (Usborne). See also the suggestions for further reading on page 42.

3: 2: W12: to recognise and generate compound words, e.g. *playground, airport, shoelace, underneath*; and to use this knowledge to support their spelling

3: 2: S6: to note where commas occur in reading and to discuss their functions in helping the reader

repetition for emphasis

⬭ᴷ = key words

comma indicates pause in reading

traditional hero

compound words

shows that they come in peace

description of Cyclops

unattractive characteristics built up

getting some idea of the cave dweller

unattractive characteristics built up

indicates that Odysseus is brave

Odysseus
Extract 1

The war was over at last. At last, after ten long years, the soldiers who had fought in it could sail home. Among them was Odysseus, King of Ithaca. He and his men rowed out to sea on their ship the *Odyssey*, leaving the battlefields far behind them.

There was little room aboard for food and water, but some huge jugs of wine stood in the prow, taken from the defeated enemy. Unfortunately, the first time they tasted it, the men fell asleep over their oars. "A bit too strong," decided Odysseus, watching them snore. Then a storm overtook them and blew them off course—to an island, who knows where?

Odysseus pointed up at a cliff. "I'm sure those caves up there are inhabited. Let's climb up and ask for directions and a bite to eat. Leave your swords here, and bring a jug of wine, to show we're friendly."

The first cave they came to was huge and smelled of cheese. But nobody was in. A fire burned in one corner. The soldiers sat down and waited. Soon there was a clatter of hoofs on the cliff path, as the island shepherd drove his flock home from the fields to the caves. And what sheep entered the cave! They were as big as cows, with fleeces like snowdrifts.

But the shepherd made his sheep look tiny. He was as big as the wooden horse of Troy, and his hair hung down like creepers. A single eye winked in the centre of his forehead. He rolled a massive boulder across the cave mouth, then turned and saw his visitors.

"Supper!" he roared, in delight. And picking up a man in each paw, he gobbled them down and spat out their belts and sandals.

"Sir! We came to you in peace! How dare you eat my men!" cried Odysseus, more angry than afraid.

3: 2: S7: to use the term 'comma' appropriately in relation to reading

3: 2: T3: to identify and discuss main and recurring characters, evaluate their behaviour and justify views

3: 2: T6: to plan main points as a structure for story writing, considering how to capture points in a few words that can be elaborated later; discuss different methods of planning

3: 2: T8: to write portraits of characters, using story text to describe behaviour and characteristics, and presenting portraits in a variety of ways, e.g. as posters, labelled diagrams, letters to friends about them

3: 2: T10: to write alternative sequels to traditional stories using same characters and settings

Odysseus

by Geraldine McCaughrean

Extract 2

Background

This second extract about Odysseus continues directly on from the first. The Cyclops has returned to the cave and has just eaten two of Odysseus' friends. In this extract, Odysseus reveals his heroic qualities by playing a clever trick on the Cyclops and in doing so manages to save the lives of himself and his friends.

Shared reading and discussing the text

● Remind the children of the first extract about Odysseus, which started the story. Remind the children that this story is about the hero Odysseus and is one adventure on a journey that takes him ten years to complete.

● Read the text and ask the children to explain what Odysseus does in the story that encourages the reader to see him as a hero and why he and his companions are able to work together so successfully.

● With the children, think about other heroes they have read about and explore what qualities a hero might have.

● Read the text again, explaining how the use of punctuation helps the reader make sense of the text. Choose five children to read the excerpt taking on different parts (the Cyclops, Odysseus, Odysseus' friends, the giants and the narrator). Encourage them to read with expression using the information given by the text and the punctuation.

● Focus attention on the use of capital letters for *No One* indicating it as a person's name and ask why this is significant in the story.

● Underline the other uses of capital letters in the text and then make a list to establish the rules for using a capital letter. For example, start of a sentence, name of a person or place.

Activities

● Ask the children to imagine that they are one of the friends accompanying Odysseus on the journey home and that they are keeping a travel diary. In shared writing, model diary writing for the children, then ask them in groups to complete diary entries for the two days spent on the island and the encounter with the Cyclops. Ask them to explain how they felt when they were trapped in the cave and how frightened they might have been clinging to the sheep while the Cyclops was trying to find them. They should also include information about how Odysseus helped save them.

● Ask the children to write about another adventure Odysseus and his friends might have had on their journey home. It can contain all kinds of strange creatures and magic, just as Homer's stories did, for example vultures with women's heads, a great sucking monster in the ocean called Charybdis and so on.

● Tell the children to imagine that they are Odysseus' son waiting in Ithaca for him to return. He has been away for 20 years and nothing has been heard from him in all that time. Ask them to write about how the son would feel when Odysseus suddenly appeared. Perhaps joy would be followed by amazement that it had taken so long.

● In groups, the children could write out a poster of a set of rules for using capital letters, using this text as an example.

Extension/further reading

Read the rest of the story of Odysseus' travels after the Trojan War. Tell the children to imagine that they are Odysseus and that they are allowed to send just one message home to their family while on their way home. Specify that the message can only be 50 words long and that they have no idea how long it will be before they reach Ithaca.

Provide the children with encyclopaedias such as Encarta to find out more about the Greek myths and the characters in the stories.

3: 2: S8: other uses of capitalisation from reading, e.g. names

3: 2: T2: to identify typical story themes, e.g. trials and forfeits, good over evil, weak over strong, wise over foolish

3: 2: T3: to identify and discuss main and recurring characters, evaluate their behaviour and justify views

typical story theme: brain versus brawn

Odysseus

Extract 2

"I'm Polyphemus the Cyclops," said the one-eyed giant. "I eat who I want. Who are you?"

"I am O… I am called No One—and I demand that you let us go! Why ever did I bring a present to a man like you?"

"Present? Where? Give it! I won't eat you if you give me a present!" Odysseus pointed out the jug of wine.

Polyphemus chewed off the seal and gulped down the wine. He smacked his lips. "Good stuff, No One. Good stuff."

"So you'll roll back the boulder and let us go?"

"Oh, I wouldn't shay that," slurred the Cyclops, reeling about. "What I meant to shay wash, I won't eat you… till morning." And hooting with drunken laughter, he crashed down on his back, fast asleep.

Twelve men pushed against the boulder, but they could not roll it aside.

"We're finished, captain!" they cried.

But Odysseus was busy with the huge shepherd's crook—sharpening the end to a point with his knife. The work took all night.

Towards dawn, the sailors heated the point red-hot in the fire, lifted it to their shoulders… and charged! They plunged the crook into the Cyclops' one horrible eye.

Polyphemus woke with a scream that brought his fellow giants running.

"Polyphemus, what's wrong? Is there someone in there with you?"

"No One's in here with me!" groaned Polyphemus.

"Are you hurt, then?"

"No One has hurt me!" bellowed Polyphemus.

"Good, good," said the giants outside, and plodded back to their caves. "Perhaps he had a nightmare," they said.

Polyphemus groped about blindly. "Trickery won't save you, No One. You and your men shan't leave this cave alive!"

In the morning he rolled the boulder aside, so that his sheep could run out to the fields and feed. But he himself sat in the doorway, his hands spread to catch any Greek trying to escape.

Quickly, Odysseus told his men to cling on under the huge, woolly sheep, and although Polyphemus stroked each fleece as it came by him, he did not feel the man hanging on underneath.

So captain and crew escaped.

indicates that Odysseus is not afraid

Cyclops is slurring his speech because he is drunk

Odysseus is addressed as captain; he is the leader

powerful verbs

capital letters indicate this is a person's name

capital letter to begin a sentence

adjectives

3: 2: T8: to write portraits of characters, using story text to describe behaviour and characteristics, and presenting portraits in a variety of ways, e.g. as posters, labelled diagrams, letters to friends about them

3: 2: T9: to write a story plan for own myth, fable or traditional tale, using story theme from reading but substituting different characters or changing the setting

3: 2: T10: to write alternative sequels to traditional stories using same characters and settings

The Miller, His Son and Their Donkey

by Margaret Clark

Background

Fables are traditional tales with a moral. They were originally told thousands of years ago in countries such as Greece and Persia. The characters in fables were often animals that were given special qualities, for example the fox was usually portrayed as cunning and the lion as powerful.

Aesop is the best-known fabulist and he is thought to have been a Greek slave who lived on the island of Samos in about the 6th century BC. The fables developed as an oral tradition and the stories ascribed to Aesop were not written down until about 200 years later so it is difficult to trace their origin. It is not known if Aesop made clear the moral message in his stories: they were told to entertain and this is the emphasis put on this story retold by Margaret Clarke.

Shared reading and discussing the text

● Initially, read through the fable without comment, then tell the children that this is one example of a fable, which is a traditional story first thought to have been told by Aesop thousands of years ago. Explain the stories were not written down at first so they changed each time someone told them and made the story special to them. Fables were meant to amuse and entertain their audience, but there was also something to be learnt from the story and this is known as the moral.

● Point out to the children that there are clear themes that return in many fables, for example good triumphs over evil, the weak triumph over the strong, the wise over the foolish. Discuss other stories the children may have heard that have a moral. Can the children identify the moral/theme in this story?

● Point out to the children that many of the stories have animals as their main characters and that these animals are given human characteristics. Explain that this story has a miller as the main character.

● Explore the character of the miller with the children. Tell them that a miller is someone who grinds corn into flour and that this was an important work a long while ago.

● Read the fable again and emphasise the lines that are repeated throughout the story. Using a displayed copy of the text, explore the structure of question and response with the children.

Activities

● In shared writing, draw out the skeleton of the story as a diagram.

● Working in pairs, ask the children to take it in turns to tell the fable using the lines that are repeated throughout the story. They could then perform this to another pair.

● In group work, the children can write the story from the point of view of the donkey.

● Tell the children that they are now going to write their own fable, but the main character is going to be an animal. Ask the children to think of an animal they believe could be very foolish, for example a camel, goat or sheep. Imagine this animal is being given advice by the animals it passes on a journey. Initially, give the children a story planner to complete, which they can talk about with a partner. When they are happy with the plan, they can go on to write their story.

Extension/further reading

Provide a range of books containing fables for the children to read and discuss morals and how versions of stories differ. See, for example, other tales written by Margaret Clarke in *The Very Best of Aesop's Fables* (Walker Books) or *Aesop's Fables* retold by Malorie Blackman (Scholastic Hippo).

3: 2: T2: to identify typical story themes, e.g. trials and forfeits, good over evil, weak over strong, wise over foolish

3: 2: T3: to identify and discuss main and recurring characters, evaluate their behaviour and justify views

typical fable title

typical generic character for fable; person who grinds corn into flour

patterned structure: repeated phrase

speech marks

exclamation mark inside speech marks

The Miller, His Son and Their Donkey

A miller was driving his donkey to market. His young son trudged along behind him.

"How silly you are!" said a girl they passed on the road. "Why make your son walk when he could ride on the donkey?"

"What a good idea!" said the miller, and he lifted his son on to the donkey's back. The miller went on driving the donkey but soon he began to feel very hot.

"How silly you are!" said a friend of the miller's who came up behind them. "You spoil that son of yours. Why don't _you_ ride the donkey and make him walk?"

"What a good idea!" said the miller, lifting the boy off the donkey's back and mounting it himself. The boy soon began to trail far behind.

"How selfish you are!" said a woman sitting by the roadside. "Why don't you let the boy ride with you?"

"What a good idea!" said the miller, lifting the boy up beside him. After a while the donkey was so tired it could hardly put one foot in front of the other.

"How silly you are!" said a traveller, passing them. "If you ride that donkey all the way to market, it will be worn out when you get there, and no one will buy it. You'd better carry it and give it a rest."

"What a good idea!" said the miller. He got off the donkey and lifted his son down. Then they tied the donkey's legs together and carried it upside down on a pole. The donkey was very frightened. It kicked and struggled so much that, just as they were passing over a bridge, its ropes broke and it fell into the river. And they never saw it again.

unnamed characters; typical of fables

sudden ending

3: 2: T9: to write a story plan for own myth, fable or traditional tale, using story theme from reading but substituting different characters or changing the setting

3: 2: T10: to write alternative sequels to traditional stories using same characters and settings, identifying typical phrases and expressions from story and using these to help structure the writing

The Boy Who Cried Wolf

retold by Margaret Clark

Background

This second fable is also believed to have been first told by Aesop in about the 6th century BC. The strong oral tradition behind fables is evident here, with a simple storyline and little time taken up with setting the scene or describing characters. For example, in this fable the main character is just referred to as *a boy* and the setting as *a village*. The fable has a clear moral, but is written to entertain and this is the emphasis put on this retelling.

Shared reading and discussing the text

● Begin the session by investigating whether the children know the phrase *to cry wolf.* Then read the story and ask the children who has heard the story before. Remind them that Aesop's fables were originally told by him and not actually written down until quite recently.

● Explain that when this story was first told, more children would have known what it was like to have to work looking after sheep. The story was thus more relevant to the people it was told to at the time.

● Discuss how the villagers might feel after they had rushed to the field and found the boy laughing and why they did not come the third time. Go on to explore how the boy might feel on the different occasions. Discuss the structure of the story with the children and ask why there were two false alarms before the real attack.

● Remind the children that fables have morals and, in pairs, ask them to decide the moral for this story. Share this as a class.

● Tell the children that part of the title of this story *to cry wolf* now also has a more general meaning, that is, a person who gives a warning about an event when it is not necessary.

● Point out to the children that in this story certain parts are repeated so that the audience begins to think that they know what will come next. For example, the phrase Wolf! Wolf! is repeated twice. Tension is built up with the reader thinking that the known may become the unknown at some point, as does happen when the real wolf eventually appears.

● Point out the use of the collective noun flock. Do the children know any more collective nouns related to groups of animals, for example herd of cows, pack of wolves? What do they notice about the plural form sheep?

Activities

● In shared writing, explore the boy's different feelings on days 1, 2 and 3. Write these feelings in the boy's voice.

● Ask the children to draw a picture of the boy and write about the changes in his character at the end after learning an important lesson.

● Explain that as a class you are going to set a fable in the present day and write the text together in shared writing. Choose an experience that is relevant to their daily lives or one with a cross-curricular link. For example, being unkind to a younger brother, sister or animal; not following a school rule.

● In groups, ask the children to plan and write a fable of their own, thinking carefully about the moral. They could read or tell their story to the class and ask them what they understand to be the moral of the story. Children will often find different morals in a story, so it is helpful if they explain the reasons for their decision.

● Ask the children to draw a 'wanted poster' for a character who is in need of a lesson. The children need to write a description of the character(s) and why they are 'wanted'. They could then think of a way the character could learn a lesson and be reformed. If they are struggling for ideas, suggest they choose a familiar character from a traditional tale, such as the wolf in *Little Red Riding Hood* or the ugly sisters in *Cinderella.*

Extension/further reading

Moral tales are usually very serious but it might be fun to write a more humorous fable. Some suggestions could be: a rich, greedy man decides to share his money but every time he gives it away he gets back more than he gave away; or a boy/girl who tries to trick people by telling lies but everything they say comes true.

3: 2: S4: to extend knowledge and understanding of pluralisation through understanding the term 'collective noun' and collecting examples – experiment with inventing other collective nouns

3: 2: T2: to identify typical story themes, e.g. trials and forfeits, good over evil, weak over strong, wise over foolish

not a developed character, which is a typical feature of fables

not a developed setting

structure – plot repeated twice and then changes on the third telling

The Boy Who Cried Wolf

collective noun

a deliberate plan to deceive the villagers

A boy was sent to look after a flock of sheep as they grazed near a village. It was raining, and he was bored, so he decided to play a trick on the villagers.

"Wolf! Wolf!" he shouted as loud as he could. "There's a wolf attacking your sheep."

irregular plural

Out ran all the villagers, leaving whatever they were doing, to drive away the wolf. When they rushed into the field and found the sheep quite safe, the boy laughed and laughed.

The next day the same thing happened.

"Wolf! Wolf!" shouted the boy.

repeated phrase

And when the villagers ran into the field and again found everything quiet, he laughed more than ever. On the third day a wolf really did come.

"Wolf! Wolf!" shouted the boy, as the sheep ran wildly in all directions.

"Oh, please come quickly!"

But this time none of the villagers took any notice, because they thought he was only playing tricks, as he had done before.

moral – the lesson to be learnt

3: 2: T8: to write portraits of characters, using story text to describe behaviour and characteristics, and presenting portraits in a variety of ways, e.g. as posters, labelled diagrams, letters to friends about them

3: 2: T9: to write a story plan for own myth, fable or traditional tale, using story theme from reading but substituting different characters or changing the setting

Three Raindrops by Terry Jones

Background

This is an imaginative story that requires children to think about the meaning behind the short tale. The fable has an ending with a clear moral, as the three boastful raindrops become part of a very muddy puddle. The story also uses the number three, which is often used in traditional stories, for example the three little pigs, the three ugly sisters, three wishes and so on.

Shared reading and discussing the text

● Before reading the story, remind the children about the oral tradition of fables and traditional tales. Read the story through, then ask them if they can remember the phrase that is repeated three times – *best raindrop in the whole sky*. Ask the children to think about what effect the phrase has on the reader.

● After reading the story, explore the argument between the raindrops and link this to the use of comparative and superlative adjectives in the tale, for example *best*, *biggest*.

● Brainstorm what word or words the children would use to describe all the raindrops, for example *boastful*, *bigheaded* and so on. Then ask them to think of a reason why Terry Jones might have written the story. Discuss if they think he has made the meaning clear. Ask the children what they think the moral for the story could be, for example *Pride comes before a fall*, which in this case is literally a fall into a muddy puddle.

● Give each child a copy of the story and then put the children into groups of four and allocate each child a part of the story to read, for example narrator, first raindrop, second raindrop and third raindrop. After they have rehearsed their parts, ask two or three groups to read to the class.

● Discuss the use of the apostrophe to spell shortened forms of words in the extract. Explain that the apostrophe is used instead of the missing letter, for example *I'm, it's, you're*. Ask the children to give more examples and build up a class list.

Activities

● In 'Three Raindrops', the raindrops end up in a muddy puddle. Ask the children to write a different ending to the story, for example the drops could end up in a river, still quarrelling about who is the best, or need to combine as one big drop to save themselves from being swallowed by an animal.

● In shared writing, model writing a plan for a fable. The plan could use a writing frame with these headings *setting, characters, conflict, solution, moral* and use a similar structure to 'Three Raindrops'. Choose, for example, three snowflakes who each boast about being the most beautiful/delicate/intricate, ending with them all melting, or three trees who boast about being the tallest, the oldest or having the most leaves, ending with them all chopped down.

● Ask the children to plan and write their own version of the story you began planning in shared writing, keeping it to about the length of 'Three Raindrops'. They need to think about a line that could be repeated three times during the story. Help the children to edit and correct the story, then discuss how to develop the work for presentation in a class book.

● Divide the children into groups of four and ask them to choose one of the stories they have written for performing to the whole class or other year groups. Ask them to allocate parts, including a narrator, and act out the story.

Extension/further reading

In groups, ask the children to explore how this moral relates to their own lives and friendships. Share these thoughts as a class.

A Short Anthology of Fables retold by Janeen Brian (Era Books) provides a good range.

3: 2: S2: the function of adjectives within sentences, through:
● identifying adjectives in shared reading
● discussing and defining what they have in common i.e. words which qualify nouns

3: 2: T2: to identify typical story themes, e.g. trials and forfeits, good over evil, weak over strong, wise over foolish

Three Raindrops

A raindrop was falling out of a cloud, and it said to the raindrop next to it: "I'm the biggest and best raindrop in the whole sky!"

"You are indeed a fine raindrop," said the second, "but you are not nearly so beautifully shaped as I am. And in my opinion it's shape that counts, and *I* am therefore the best raindrop in the whole sky."

The first raindrop replied: "Let us settle this matter once and for all." So they asked a third raindrop to decide between them.

But the third raindrop said: "What nonsense you're both talking! *You* may be a big raindrop, and *you* are certainly well shaped, but, as everybody knows, it's purity that really counts, and I am purer than either of you. *I* am therefore the best raindrop in the whole sky!"

Well, before either of the other raindrops could reply, they all three hit the ground and became part of a very muddy puddle.

adjectives

use of apostrophe for contractions

phrase repeated three times

italic used for emphasis; helps reader

apostrophe could be used here

superlative

comparative

moral: pride comes before a fall

3: 2: T5: rehearse and improve performance, taking note of punctuation and meaning

3: 2: T6: to plan main points as a structure for story writing, considering how to capture points in a few words that can be elaborated later; discuss different methods of planning

3: 2: T9: to write a story plan for own myth, fable or traditional tale, using story theme from reading but substituting different characters or changing the setting

The Greedy Man

retold by Rina Singh

Extract 1

Background

Many of the traditional tales in this section come from an oral tradition. Examples of traditional stories can be found in many cultures and this extract is taken from a traditional Chinese tale with a strong moral theme. The story is of two neighbours – a farmer who is kind and generous and a greedy merchant. One day the farmer saves the life of a wounded bird and is rewarded by the bird when it is well again. He is given a pumpkin seed which when planted, produces pumpkins which are filled with gold and other riches. Overcome with jealousy, the merchant deliberately injures a bird in order to nurse it back to health. He, too, is given a pumpkin seed but when this one is planted, it grows towards the moon. The greedy merchant climbs this in order to reach the gold and silver of the moon, but is left stranded there for ever when the vine disappears.

Shared reading and discussing the text

● Conceal all but the first sentence and read this with the children. Discuss what sort of story the opening words suggest it might be. Why do we think this? (*Long ago…* is a commonly used opening in traditional tales.) Ask the children to suggest how else a traditional/folk/fairy tale might begin. For example, *Once upon a time… Many years ago… Long ago and far away…*

● Reveal the rest of the text and read from the beginning with the children. Look for and highlight other traditional elements, such as the setting (*at night, by the light of the moon*) and old-fashioned language (*kind deeds*), which link with the tale taking place *long ago.*

● Discuss the nature of the characters. Look at the second sentence and highlight the words that show the farmer was a good man (*kind, generous*). Find and list other words and phrases which support this (for example, *sharing what little he had, was fondly admired*; also *tilled* and *wove* show he worked hard). Do the same with the contrasting character of the merchant (*cunning, greedy, he'd often lie*). Show the children how the phrase *On the*

other hand tells us that the characters are very different.

● Ask the children what we call words that describe a noun (adjectives). Identify the adjectives in the story and discuss what they do.

● Ask the children if they can identify any synonyms within the text (for example *provisions* and *products*). Can they think of any others that might be substituted for these (*supplies/groceries*)?

● Re-read the text with the children and ask them to predict what happens next.

Activities

● In pairs, ask the children to discuss and list other traditional stories with contrasting characters. (Obvious examples include 'Cinderella' and 'Snow White'.)

● In groups, ask children to make collections of adjectives to describe contrasting characters (for example, *good/bad, kind/mean, rich/poor*) and present these as spider diagrams or as a word bank to support class story writing.

● Help the children to experiment with substituting new adjectives, or deleting existing ones in the text and note the effect on meaning.

● In guided writing groups, ask the children to predict and write the next part of the story. Encourage them to continue the use of traditional story style in their writing.

Extension/further reading

Make a collection of other traditional stories with similar themes and compare their use of language, style, structure and so on. For example, *Mufaro's Beautiful Daughters* by John Steptoe (Hodder and Stoughton) tells the tale of two daughters – one selfish, the other kind – who are rivals for the king's hand in marriage. *Chinye* by Obi Onyefulu and Evie Safarewicz (Frances Lincoln) is a West African folk tale that contrasts the goodness of Chinye against the greed and callousness of her stepmother and stepsister.

3: 2: S2: the function of adjectives within sentences, through:
● identifying adjectives in shared reading
● discussing and defining what they have in common i.e. words which qualify nouns
● experimenting with deleting and substituting adjectives and noting effects on meaning
● collecting and classifying adjectives, e.g. for colours, sizes, moods
● experimenting with the impact of different adjectives through shared writing

3: 2: S3: to use the term 'adjective' appropriately

markedly contrasting characters – a dominant feature/ theme of many traditional stories

typical opening style for traditional story

The Greedy Man *Extract 1*

In long ago China, in a small village by a river, lived two neighbours. One of them was a kind and generous man. He was a farmer, who tilled the little rice field he had inherited from his father. At night, by the light of the moon, he wove straw baskets to sell in the market. Although he worked very hard, he never managed to have any money left over for extras or to put away for his old age. But that didn't stop him from sharing what little he had with other people in need. He was fondly admired by all the villagers for his many kind deeds.

The farmer's neighbour, on the other hand, was cunning and greedy. He made his living as a merchant, riding into town to buy all sorts of provisions such as tea, salt and fresh fish. When he returned to the village he would sell them to the villagers at a good profit. He'd often lie to the villagers about the true price of some products or the scarcity of others. "I've heard rumours that there will be no more salt in the market for a few months," he would tell them most dramatically, after his return from town. Word would spread though the village and people would line up in front of his store and buy all his salt.

adjectives to describe character

traditional tasks

traditional story language

old-fashioned language links with story taking place 'long ago'

adjectives to describe merchant's character

phrase emphasises contrasting characters

builds up picture of greedy man

separate paragraphs to contrast 2 very different characters

synonyms

shortage

3: 2: T1: to investigate the styles and voices of traditional story language – collect examples, e.g. story openings and endings; scene openers, e.g. *'Now when...', 'A long time ago...'*; list, compare and use in own writing

3: 2: T2: to identify typical story themes, e.g. trials and forfeits, good over evil, weak over strong, wise over foolish

3: 2: T8: to write portraits of characters, using story text to describe behaviour and characteristics, and presenting portraits in a variety of ways

3: 2: T10: to write alternative sequels to traditional stories using same characters and settings, identifying typical phrases and expressions from story and using these to help structure the writing

The Greedy Man

retold by Rina Singh

Extract 2

Background

This second extract from 'The Greedy Man' develops the next stage of the story. The farmer saves the life of a wounded bird and when the bird is set free, it promises to return with a reward for the farmer. All the stories in Rina Singh's book *Moon Tales* attempt to help explain the mysteries of the moon. In this tale, the moon becomes a place where people are sent for punishment.

Shared reading and discussing the text

● Read the first passage again. Remind the children what we know about the nature of the merchant that made him unpopular in the village. Now read the second extract.

● Once read, investigate what else the children have learnt about the two characters from reading this extract. While discussing the characters, try to make further comparisons between the two.

● Ask the children how the farmer tried to be a friendly neighbour to the merchant. Discuss other ways the farmer might have attempted to be neighbourly.

● Discuss with the children how the farmer looked after the little brown sparrow. Point out that it is only because the farmer is kind and expected nothing in return that he is offered a reward by the bird. Read the text carefully and identify how the author tells us of the farmer's kindness.

● Explore with the children why the author chose such an ordinary bird for the farmer to save – a more beautiful or rarer bird might have been more glamorous, but would not have made the farmer's altruistic intentions as clear.

● Point out that in many traditional stories animals do speak, and ask the children if they can give other examples of this. Discuss how the inclusion of a creature (in this case, a bird) with the ability to grant rewards for good behaviour (and punishment for bad) is also an element common to traditional tales.

● Ask the children what kind of reward they think the bird might give the farmer. Point out

that the bird will probably give something that will be suitable for a farmer. When the children have given their suggestions, tell them that the bird returned with a pumpkin seed, which the farmer planted and when it had grown it produced pumpkins full of gold.

● Point out to the children that in traditional tales kind, good behaviour is often rewarded, and unkind, bad behaviour is often punished. Briefly tell them the outcome of the story where the greedy merchant is left stranded on the moon for ever.

Activities

● In pairs, ask the children to write two headings, *The merchant* and *The farmer*, and under the correct heading note down the characteristics of the two figures, for example *greedy* and *kind*. Then ask the children to provide evidence for this from the story, for example *he often lied to the villagers by pretending that there was a shortage of a product*.

● Remind the children of the predictions they made earlier for continuing the story, then ask them to write the story with their own interpretation of a reward for the kind farmer. Encourage them to use the language of traditional stories.

● In pairs, ask the children to discuss how they think the greedy man in the story came to be stranded on the moon for ever. Then ask them to write this part of the story.

Extension/further reading

Ask the children to write down the names of good and bad characters from stories they know, then choose one of the characters and write a character sketch, explaining why they acted in the way they did. Read 'Why the Moon Waxes and Wanes', which comes from the same book as 'The Greedy Man' – *Moon Tales* by Rina Singh (Bloomsbury). This story comes from Australia. The children could write their own traditional tale to explain the moon's appearance and disappearance.

3: 2: T1: to investigate the styles and voices of traditional story language – collect examples, e.g. story openings and endings; scene openers, e.g. *'Now when...'*, *'A long time ago...'*; list, compare and use in own writing

3: 2: T2: to identify typical story themes, e.g. trials and forfeits, good over evil, weak over strong, wise over foolish

The Greedy Man

Extract 2

Although people in the village didn't care for the merchant, the farmer tried to be friendly with his neighbour. They often did neighbourly things together, such as survey each other's vegetable gardens. Sometimes they had tea together and went on walks on long summer evenings.

examples of neighbourly activities and kindness of farmer

One evening, as they were walking along a riverbank, they saw a wounded bird. The little brown sparrow was wet and injured and its little body was throbbing with pain. The kind man stopped to pick it up and stroked its dishevelled feathers.

adjectives describing bird

"Why do you bother with a creature that is half dead? It will be nothing but a nuisance to you," said the greedy man impatiently. It was beginning to get dark and a new moon was rising. He was hungry for his supper and eager to get home.

examples of attitude of greedy man

"You go on ahead," said the kind man, gently carrying the bird in the folds of his sleeve. He brought it home and wrapped it up in an old shirt and placed it in a box near the window. He cared for the bird every day and talked to it as if it were a little child. He applied a splint to its broken wing and fed it every day. He became so fond of the bird, the thought of parting with it was painful to him. However, when the bird was well and the wing had healed, he knew he must let it go. One beautiful morning he came out of the house with the bird perched on his hand.

hint of things to come?

more examples of the farmer's kindness

contrast in adverbs describing characters' speech

"Go, little one, fly home," he said, ever so tenderly.

And then a very odd thing happened. The bird spoke.

short sentence for dramatic effect

The kind man was startled to hear the bird say, "You were so kind to me and you expected nothing in return. I shall come back with a reward for you." Saying this, the bird flew across the rice paddies.

3: 2: T8: to write portraits of characters, using story text to describe behaviour and characteristics, and presenting portraits in a variety of ways

3: 2: T10: to write alternative sequels to traditional stories using same characters and settings, identifying typical phrases and expressions from story and using these to help structure the writing

The Magic Porridge Pot

retold by Jackie Andrews

Background

This well-known tale has been retold by Jackie Andrews from a version by the Grimm brothers, who published their collection of German fairy stories in 1857. Andrews' modern retelling has all the ingredients of a traditional story: it begins with the words *There was once*, introduces a little girl and her mother who are very poor, a mysterious old woman saves them from starvation with some magical intervention, two simple phrases are repeated three times and the story concludes with the traditional happy ending, although there is a problem along the way.

Shared reading and discussing the text

● Read up to where the little girl says *I'm trying to find some nuts and berries*. Cover the rest of the story. Ask the children to predict what might happen next, then read the rest of the story. Compare the children's predictions with what actually happens.
● Focus the children's attention on reading the story using appropriate voices and expression. Notice the use of punctuation marks.
● Discuss what features identify this as a traditional tale, such as the story opening, a poor girl and her mother, the introduction of a magic pot and a happy ending.
● Discuss how sympathy for the *little/poor* girl and *thin/hungry* mother is influenced by this choice of adjectives.
● Read the story, annotating the text using the following headings: *setting, problem, solution*.
● Encourage the class to think of other stories that use magical objects, for example the bean in 'Jack and the Beanstalk', the Golden Goose.

Activities

● Ask pairs of children to retell the story to each other. Split the story into four parts and ask the children to tell each part separately – girl meets old woman who gives her a magic pot; girl demonstrates to mother how the pot works; mother uses pot with disastrous consequences; girl returns to save situation and so generates

happy ending. Emphasise to the children that they are retelling the story *orally* and that this is how stories were told a long time ago.
● Ask the children to design, draw and then write their own description of a magic pot, including information about what it is made from, what magic it can perform and instructions about its use.
● Point out the three occurrences of *Cook, little pot, cook!* and *Stop, little pot, stop!* and that the number three is used frequently in traditional stories. In groups, ask the children to discuss and list all the stories they know that use this special number. (For example, 'The Three Little Pigs', 'The Three Raindrops'.)
● In shared writing, point out that this story is told in the third person. Model writing the story in the first person from the point of view of the little girl, her mother or the old woman. The children can then carry on in their groups.
● Using the headings elaborated on earlier as prompts – *setting, problem, solution* – ask the children to write their own traditional story. Versions of their story could be reworked as a handwriting exercise, illustrated, made into a book and then read with appropriate expression to the class or other year groups.
● Provide the children with a copy of the text with some of the adjectives underlined and ask them to replace these with synonyms. Then ask the children to find suitable antonyms.
● Divide the class into groups of four and allocate the parts of the little girl, her mother, the old woman and narrator and ask them to read the extract. Then remove the text and ask them to act out the story using their own words to convey the meaning.

Extension/further reading

Read or tell another of the Grimm brothers' tales such as 'Hansel and Gretel', 'Snow White' or 'Rumpelstiltskin' and ask the children to write their own version of the story. There are some excellent versions of the Grimm tales in *Rumpelstiltskin and other Grimm Tales* told by Carol Ann Duffy (Faber and Faber).

3: 2: S2: the function of adjectives within sentences, through:
● identifying adjectives in shared reading
● discussing and defining what they have in common i.e. words which qualify nouns
● experimenting with deleting and substituting adjectives and noting effects on meaning
● collecting and classifying adjectives, e.g. for colours, sizes, moods
● experimenting with the impact of different adjectives through shared writing

3: 2: S3: to use the term 'adjective' appropriately

typical traditional story opening

part 1: problem established

part 2: solution offered

part 3: crisis

part 4: happy ending

simple characters, not developed

setting

adjectives

commas and punctuation aid reading and improve meaning

phrases occur 3 times

The Magic Porridge Pot

1 There was once a little girl and her mother who were so poor that the little girl had to go out into the nearby wood to search for nuts and berries to eat. While she was there, she met an old woman.

"My!" said the little old woman. "You look very thin and hungry, dear!"

2 "My mother and I have no food," the little girl explained. "I'm trying to find some nuts and berries."

"Here, take this," said the old woman. She gave the little girl a small, iron cooking pot. "When you want a meal, just say, 'Cook, little pot, cook!' It will fill with hot porridge. When you've had enough, just say, 'Stop, little pot, stop!'"

Delighted, the little girl thanked the old woman, ran home with the pot and put it on the kitchen table in front of her astonished mother.

"Cook, little pot, cook!" she said, and immediately the pot filled with bubbly, hot porridge. The little girl and her mother ate until they were full. Then the little girl said "Stop, little pot, stop!" and the pot stopped cooking. She and her mother hugged each other and laughed. They would never be hungry again!

3 Next day, while the little girl was visiting a friend, the mother took out the cooking pot. "Cook, little pot, cook!" she said, and the pot began to fill with lovely, hot porridge. The mother ate as much as she wanted, then had a nap by the fireside.

But the little cooking pot went on cooking. Soon the whole cottage was filled with porridge. Porridge poured down the hillside and into the village. Then the whole village was filled with porridge. And still the little cooking pot went on cooking.

4 Just then, the little girl came home. What a sight met her!

"Stop, little pot, stop!" she cried. And at last the pot stopped cooking.

The little girl and her mother – and everyone in the village – had enough porridge to last them a lifetime.

3: 2: S6: to note where commas occur in reading and to discuss their functions in helping the reader

3: 2: T1: to investigate the styles and voices of traditional story language – collect examples, e.g. story openings and endings; scene openers, e.g. *'Now when...', 'A long time ago...'*; list, compare and use in own writing

3: 2: T9: to write a story plan for own myth, fable or traditional tale, using story theme from reading but substituting different characters or changing the setting

The Story of the Mirror and its Fragments

by Hans Christian Andersen

Background

Hans Christian Andersen was a Danish author who lived during the 19th century (1805–75). He wrote and collected more than 150 stories for children. He was one of the first children's authors to use a style and content that introduced children to ideas and language at one time thought to be beyond their understanding. Among the most famous stories he wrote are *The Ugly Duckling*, *The Emperor's New Clothes*, *The Red Shoes*, *The Little Mermaids* and *The Snow Queen*, from which this extract comes.

The Snow Queen is about a boy called Kay and a girl called Gerda and how a fragment of mirror entered Kay's heart allowing him to be carried away by the Snow Queen. The story tells of Gerda's determined search to find Kay and release him from his ice prison. This extract starts the story and explains how the mirror fragments came to exist and how the splinters could enter the eye and heart and make it become *cold and hard, like a lump of ice*.

Shared reading and discussing the text

● Tell the children that this is the start of a traditional story written by Hans Christian Andersen nearly 200 years ago. Ask the children if they know any other stories by him.
● Read the extract and point out to the children that traditional stories usually have good and bad characters. Ask the children who they think these are in this story. Explore how the author gives the reader a clear indication of the character of a troll, for example he laughs and is proud at his clever work of making beautiful things odious.
● Discuss the ending of the extract with the children, which talks about *seeing everything the wrong way.* Explain that this is a figurative use of language and means that the fragments of glass brought out the worst in people and caused them to act in the worst possible way. Give the children an example, such as mimicking people's worst habits, saying unkind things. Ask them to add their own ideas.

● Explain the meanings of unfamiliar words and suggest ways of working out the meanings of words by reading them in context.

Activities

● Provide a copy of the extract and ask the children to underline the adjectives and then substitute alternatives. Discuss whether their alternative adjectives have the same impact, for example a *bad* troll instead of a *wicked* troll.
● In shared writing, ask the children to imagine that fragments of the mirror have entered their eyes and caused them to behave in an unpleasant way. Write one or two things they might do on the board, for example say unpleasant things to a friend, pull some flowers out of someone's garden. In groups, ask them to plan this as a story with a happy ending with the glass being removed by a good character.
● Using a list of nouns, such as *head*, *body*, *hands*, encourage the children to contribute adjectives to describe a troll, for example *huge*, *hairless head*; *knarled*, *stooping body*. In pairs, ask the children to write a fuller description of their own imagined troll, using this range of adjectives and nouns to help them.
● Tell the children that they are going to design a wanted poster for the troll. First they must draw the troll they have imagined and then explain his crime, for example constructing a mirror that turned good to evil.
● In shared writing, brainstorm other bad characters from traditional stories and ask the children to think about why they are bad.

Extension/further reading

We are told that the goblins studied at the school of magic. Tell the children that they have an opportunity to study at this school. What would they like to learn?

Finish reading the story of the Snow Queen, and ask the children to write an account of how Gerda saved her friend Kay.

Read more Hans Christian Andersen stories, for example *Stories from Hans Christian Andersen* retold by Andrew Matthews (Orchard).

3: 2: S2: the function of adjectives within sentences, through:
- identifying adjectives in shared reading
- discussing and defining what they have in common i.e. words which qualify nouns
- experimenting with deleting and substituting adjectives and noting effects on meaning
- collecting and classifying adjectives, e.g. for colours, sizes, moods
- experimenting with the impact of different adjectives through shared writing

3: 2: S3: to use the term 'adjective' appropriately

THE STORY OF THE MIRROR AND ITS FRAGMENTS

typical traditional story opening

traditional character

in a good mood

impact of different adjectives; can be substituted with alternatives

disgusting

twisted out of usual shape

traditional characters

There was once a wicked troll who was more wicked than anybody else. One day he was in a very happy frame of mind for he had just constructed a mirror which made everything good and beautiful shrink up to nothing when it was reflected in it, but all those things that were ugly and useless were magnified and made to appear ten times worse than before. In this mirror, the loveliest landscapes looked like boiled spinach and the most beautiful people appeared odious. Their features were so distorted that their friends could never have recognised them. Moreover, if one of them had a freckle it seemed to spread right over his nose and mouth; and if a good thought glanced across his mind, a wrinkle was seen in the mirror. The troll thought all this was highly entertaining, and he chuckled at his clever work.

The goblins who studied at the school of magic where he taught, spread the fame of this wonderful mirror, and said that for the first time the world and its inhabitants could be seen as they really were. They carried the mirror from place to place, until at last there was no country or person that had not been misrepresented in it. Then they flew up to the sky with it, to see if they could carry on their fun there. But the higher they flew the more wrinkled the mirror became; they could scarcely hold it together. They flew on and on, higher and higher, until at last the mirror trembled so much that it escaped from their hands and fell to the earth, breaking into a million, billion little pieces. And then it caused far greater unhappiness than before for fragments of it scarcely as large as a grain of sand flew about in the air, and got into people's eyes, making them see everything the wrong way…

small pieces

the people who live there

shown in a false way

barely/only just

figurative language

3: 2: T1: to investigate the styles and voices of traditional story language – collect examples, e.g. story openings and endings; scene openers, e.g. *'Now when…', 'A long time ago…';* list, compare and use in own writing

3: 2: T3: to identify and discuss main and recurring characters, evaluate their behaviour and justify views

3: 2: T8: to write portraits of characters, using story text to describe behaviour and characteristics, and presenting portraits in a variety of ways, e.g. as posters, labelled diagrams, letters to friends about them

3: 2: T9: to write a story plan for own myth, fable or traditional tale, using story theme from reading but substituting different characters or changing the setting

Tall Tales

by Valerie Bloom

Background

Some poems are meant to be performed – away from the page they come to life. This poem is one of two poems by Valerie Bloom (see also 'The River' on page 20). Valerie Bloom was born in Jamaica but later studied in Britain and her poems reflect both parts of her background, many of them written in Jamaican dialect. She started by writing stories but once she discovered the 'rhythms and feelings' in poetry, started writing in this form. 'Tall Tales' is clearly written for performance, its meaning and mood become clearer when it is spoken, enhancing appreciation of the poem.

Shared reading and discussing the text

● Read the poem with expression to the children. Go over the poem and illustrate how the reader's voice changes at certain points.
● Why do the children think it is called 'Tall Tales'? Discuss the meaning of the phrase as unbelievable things or unlikely stories.
● Read through the poem again with the class. Read the main verses yourself and ask the children to read the lines in italic. Then vice versa. Try to perfect the performance and ask the children which version they like best.
● Ask the children why they think the poet has chosen to write about a mermaid, a rolling-calf and the devil. Lead them to realise that because these are not usually seen by people and are fantastical, it increases feelings of disbelief.
● Ask the children to look at the final verse. Do they think this verse conjures up the same feelings of fantasy? Do they notice the change in language and subject as the poet moves from fantasy to the mundane and the everyday?
● Go back and explore the poem in more detail, asking the children to identify the adjectives in the first verse (*silver, green, purple*) and encourage them to see how their use increases the visual impact of the verse. Try reading the verse to the children, omitting the adjectives to demonstrate what difference this makes.
● Then, ask the children to find the rhymes in the poem and highlight them. (The second and fourth lines in each verse all rhyme – *hair/wear, toes/nose, light/night, card/yard.*)
● Discuss why the poet chooses to repeat certain words and phases, for example *I saw, you never*, and what this does for the reader and the performance.
● Read the final verse and ask children what creates the surprise and humour. Then go on to practise saying *You did!?* in different ways.

Activities

● Organise the children into mixed-ability groups to prepare the poem for performance. Encourage them to experiment with expression, tone and volume, such as reading the poem quite slowly to paint a word picture, adopting a tone of disbelief for *No, you never*, or reading the second *you never* more loudly.
● In shared writing, model writing an additional verse using the same structure and format. For example, *I saw a scary giant...*
● Ask the children to work independently or in pairs to write their own alternative verse. Encourage the use of adjectives. More confident children could begin their lines with *I heard/felt* and so on. Provide less confident children with the first two or three lines, for example:

I saw a starving monster
With red and orange eyes
I saw it eating fatty chips
And...

Then, ask the children to perform their verses to one another.

Extension/further reading

Read other poems by Valerie Bloom from her collection *Let Me Touch the Sky* (Macmillan Children's Books), for example 'My Sister...' or 'Enjoy the Party', and ask children to prepare one for performance.

Look at 'Who Dat Girl' and 'Granny Is...', also from *Let Me Touch the Sky*, which have a more obvious Caribbean influence, and make a class glossary of Jamaican dialect words used.

3: 2: S2: the function of adjectives within sentences, through:
- identifying adjectives in shared reading
- collecting and classifying adjectives, e.g. for colours, sizes, moods
- experimenting with the impact of different adjectives through shared writing

3: 2: S6: to note where commas occur in reading and to discuss their functions in helping the reader

3: 2: S8: other uses of capitalisation from reading, e.g. names, headings, special emphasis, new lines in poetry

Tall Tales

strong regular beat in each verse adds pace, particularly when spoken aloud

adjectives for colour

I saw a silver mermaid
With green and purple hair,[2]
I saw her sitting by the river
In her underwear.[4]

2nd and 4th lines of each verse rhyme

No, you never, you never.

repetition of 'never' for emphasis and rhythm

I did.

capital letters for each new line of poem

I saw a rolling-calf
With twenty-seven toes,
I saw the smoke and fire
That was coming from its nose.

progressively becoming more fantastical

No, you never, you never.

commas aid rhythm (especially in performance)

I did.

I saw the devil dancing reggae
In the bright moonlight,
I saw him sting a donkey
With his tail the other night.

repetition of 'I saw…' enhances rhythm and increases feeling of improbability

No, you never, you never.

change of language to the mundane and ordinary

I did.

italic used to indicate change of voice/tone

I saw your father busy
Reading your report card,
I saw him looking for you
All around the yard.

exclamation mark – realisation of what is being said; informs expression when speaking

full stop instead of comma differs from other verses; indicates pause

No, you never. You never! You did!?

double punctuation: poetic licence

Valerie Bloom

3: 2: T4: to choose and prepare poems for performance, identifying appropriate expression, tone, volume and use of voices and other sounds

3: 2: T5: rehearse and improve performance, taking note of punctuation and meaning

3: 2: T11: to write new or extended verses for performance based on models of 'performance' and oral poetry read, e.g. rhythms, repetition

The Dragon Who Ate Our School

by Nick Toczek

Background

Nick Toczek travels all over Britain as a poet, magician, storyteller and puppeteer. His favourite word is *suddenly* and he believes ideas come to him when he experiments with words and sees how they fit together. He believes it is very important to do some writing every day and he has stuck to this rule for more than 35 years. 'The Dragon Who Ate Our School' contains a popular and humorous theme set in the familiar environment of school. It has a strong rhyming pattern and clear structure with a chorus. The poem's familiar and accessible language (*cool, Me and my mates*) should encourage those children who sometimes find the language of poetry remote to see poetry as an enjoyable and fun experience. A poem which relishes the humour in the situation of a dragon biting *off the head of the head* but spitting out *the dinner ladies' veg and meat* will certainly appeal to Year 3 children!

Shared reading and discussing the text

● Model reading the poem to the children, indicating where you pause, and so on. Then discuss with them if they enjoyed it and why this was so.
● Discuss with the children who they think is the narrator. Explore what the narrator feels about the dragon and how they know this.
● Point out to the children that the vocabulary used in the poem provides links with children's spoken language. Give them some examples of this and encourage them to find others.
● Explain and demonstrate the importance of commas when reading aloud.
● Divide the class into six groups and give each group a verse. Initially encourage them to rehearse their verse and then perform the whole poem together as a class, each group reciting their rehearsed verse.
● Ask the children to think about which part or verse they especially liked and why.
● The children could imagine what the dragon looks like and think of words and phrases to describe her appearance and character.

● Explore with the children the pattern of rhyme and structure of the poem. Collect examples of groups of rhyming words on the board. Point out that there is some internal rhyme, for example *fed* and *red* in verse 3, and ask the children to find other examples.

Activities

● In shared writing, model writing an additional verse to insert between verses four and five. First, ask the class to suggest other activities that the dragon could be involved in, for example wrecking havoc in a PE lesson or munching her way through the Numeracy Hour. Then brainstorm a group of rhyming words to include in your verse.
● In groups, ask the children to write another verse for the poem. Encourage them to think of the rhyme and structure.
● Look at the chorus together and ask the children to write a different chorus for the poem, with a similar structure. Then ask the children to read the poem with their new verses and try out a variety of chorus suggestions.
● Divide the class into groups of three or four and provide a range of musical instruments to include in a performance of the poem. Provide tape recorders so the children can record and listen to their performance before presenting it to the class.
● Select another title, for example 'The Frog Who Ate Our Pond' or 'The Bird Who Ate Our House' and ask the children to write a humorous poem using the same format of five rhyming lines and a chorus.

Extension/further reading

The children could write a different style of poem about Nick Toczek's dragon. It could include what she looks like and what she enjoys eating.

Other performance poems include 'What Teachers Wear in Bed!' by Brian Moses and 'There's a Monster in the Garden' by David Harmer, both available in *The Works* edited by Paul Cookson (Macmillan Children's Books).

3: 2: S6: to note where commas occur in reading and to discuss their functions in helping the reader

3: 2: S7: to use the term 'comma' appropriately in relation to reading

importance of commas for reading poem out loud

examples of spoken language

short sentences for emphasis

internal rhyme

repeated chorus

structure: 5-line verse with rhymes at end of each line

different word begins chorus each time

examples of spoken language

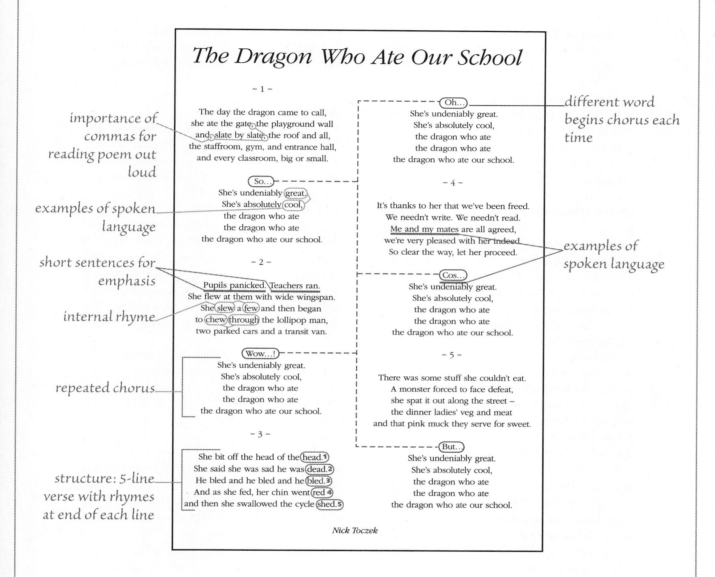

The Dragon Who Ate Our School

~ 1 ~

The day the dragon came to call,
she ate the gate, the playground wall
and, slate by slate, the roof and all,
the staffroom, gym, and entrance hall,
and every classroom, big or small.

So...
She's undeniably great.
She's absolutely cool,
the dragon who ate
the dragon who ate
the dragon who ate our school.

~ 2 ~

Pupils panicked. Teachers ran.
She flew at them with wide wingspan.
She slew a few and then began
to chew through the lollipop man,
two parked cars and a transit van.

Wow...!
She's undeniably great.
She's absolutely cool,
the dragon who ate
the dragon who ate
the dragon who ate our school.

~ 3 ~

She bit off the head of the head. 1
She said she was sad he was dead. 2
He bled and he bled and he bled. 3
And as she fed, her chin went red 4
and then she swallowed the cycle shed. 5

Oh...
She's undeniably great.
She's absolutely cool,
the dragon who ate
the dragon who ate
the dragon who ate our school.

~ 4 ~

It's thanks to her that we've been freed.
We needn't write. We needn't read.
Me and my mates are all agreed,
we're very pleased with her indeed.
So clear the way, let her proceed.

Cos...
She's undeniably great.
She's absolutely cool,
the dragon who ate
the dragon who ate
the dragon who ate our school.

~ 5 ~

There was some stuff she couldn't eat.
A monster forced to face defeat,
she spat it out along the street –
the dinner ladies' veg and meat
and that pink muck they serve for sweet.

But...
She's undeniably great.
She's absolutely cool,
the dragon who ate
the dragon who ate
the dragon who ate our school.

Nick Toczek

3: 2: T4: to choose and prepare poems for performance, identifying appropriate expression, tone, volume and use of voices and other sounds

3: 2: T5: rehearse and improve performance, taking note of punctuation and meaning

3: 2: T11: to write new or extended verses for performance based on models of 'performance' and oral poetry read, e.g. rhythms, repetition

The Boneyard Rap

by Wes Magee

Background

This is the second poem by Wes Magee included in this book (see page 34). A rap is a performance poem based on a strong rhythm, fast pace and the use of repetition. It is particularly associated with Caribbean and African-American cultures. In 'The Boneyard Rap' Wes Magee uses these characteristics clearly and children will be encouraged to participate in both the actions and words.

Shared reading and discussing the text

● Provide copies of the poem for all the children and then read it, tapping out the beat, encouraging them to join in at any point they wish. Ask the children if they can identify the form of the poem, that is a rap.

● Ask the children if they can explain what a rap is. They should emphasise the need for a strong rhythm and rhyme, together with the repetition of words and pace of presentation.

● Explain to the children that the poem has a definite structure and encourage them to discover this for themselves. Can they see that one verse is repeated (as chorus) and that every other verse begins with the lines *This is the rhythm/of the boneyard rap*? Can they work out which verse would come next?

● Can the children find the rhyming words and do they see the ABCB rhyming pattern? Ask them to put the words into rhyming groups.

● Ask the children what gesture or mime they could use to accompany the *Woooooooooo!* when performing the poem. What other gestures and mimes could they perform for other lines of the poem?

● Tell the children that *Woooooooooo!* is onomatopoeia – the word resembles the sound it makes. Can they find other examples in the poem? (For example, *click, clap, rattle*.)

● Tell the children that the commas and full stops in the poem help the performer to read the poem and give it a rhythm. Demonstrate this by reading the first verse.

● Conduct the children in a performance of the poem, using hand signals that they need to follow, for example raising/lowering your hand for louder/softer. Encourage the children to also incorporate the gestures they thought of to accompany some of the lines.

Activities

● Organise the children into groups of two to four and ask them to prepare the rap for a performance to the class. Encourage them to include musical instruments in their performance and, if possible, provide them with tape recorders so they have an opportunity to hear and improve their own efforts.

● In shared writing, brainstorm other bones or parts of the body for possible use in another verse of 'The Boneyard Rap', for example skull, tummy. Then ask them to suggest suitable actions, for example *tummy/wobble*. The children can write additional lines or verses, incorporating these words.

● Discuss with the children another subject for a rap which could start with the lines:

This is the rhythm
Of the farmyard rap
Cockerels crow

and so on. When the subject has been decided, build up a class list of words for subjects and actions, including rhyming words. Remind the children to use onomatopoeia and alliteration in their choice of words. Model the writing of the first verse with the whole class, then put the children into pairs or small groups to think up more verses. They can then perform their favourite verse to the class.

Extension/further reading

Some children might be interested in the correct names for the bones in the body and they could research these and write a scientifically accurate rap.

'In the Misty, Murky Graveyard' in *Nibbling the Page* selected by Wes Magee (Longman) is also an excellent performance poem and continues the skeleton theme.

3: 2: S6: to note where commas occur in reading and to discuss their functions in helping the reader

3: 2: S7: to use the term 'comma' appropriately in relation to reading

The Boneyard Rap

onomatopoeia

alliteration

This is the rhythm
of the boneyard rap,
knuckle bones click
and hand bones clap,
finger bones flick
and thigh bones slap,
when you're doing the rhythm
of the boneyard rap.
    Woooooooooooooo!

repeated verse/ chorus

It's the boneyard rap
and it's a scare.
Give your bones a shake-up
if you dare.
Rattle your teeth
and waggle your jaw
and let's do the boneyard rap
once more.

This is the rhythm
of the boneyard rap,
elbow bones clink
and backbones snap,
shoulder bones chink
and toe bones tap,

when you're doing the rhythm
of the boneyard rap.
    Woooooooooooooo!

It's the boneyard rap
and it's a scare.[R]
Give your bones a shake-up
if you dare.[R]
Rattle your teeth
and waggle your jaw[R]
and let's do the boneyard rap
once more.[R]

rhyme

This is the rhythm
of the boneyard rap,
ankle bones sock
and arm bones flap,
pelvic bones knock
and knee bones zap,
when you're doing the rhythm
of the boneyard rap.
    Woooooooooooooo!

repeated lines

Wes Magee

3: 2: T4: to choose and prepare poems for performance, identifying appropriate expression, tone, volume and use of voices and other sounds

3: 2: T5: rehearse and improve performance, taking note of punctuation and meaning

3: 2: T11: to write new or extended verses for performance based on models of 'performance' and oral poetry read, e.g. rhythms, repetition

Chicken Dinner

by Valerie Bloom

Background

This is the second poem by Valerie Bloom included in this section on oral and performance poetry from different cultures (see page 62). 'Chicken Dinner' is written using Jamaican dialect and accent such as *de* for 'the' and *dat* for 'that'. It is about a situation that most children will not have experienced, but the language used, feelings expressed and humour of the poem should be accessible to the children.

Shared reading and discussing the text

● Explain to the children that they are going to look at a poem written in Jamaican dialect, and provide a copy for each child to see as you read the poem. Read the first three verses and stop. Discuss the children's feelings/responses so far. Then read the last verse and compare their responses now. Discuss the sudden trick ending.

● Identify with the children whose voice they hear in the poem and to whom that voice is speaking.

● Ask the children to find examples of words and lines in Jamaican dialect. Discuss the meaning of lines such as *We know dat chicken from she hatch*. Ask the children what the *dat* is replacing.

● Discuss with the children other reasons they could give for saving the chicken's life. Record these so they can be used to write a further verse of the poem. (See Activities below.)

● Ask the children to point out the refrain (the first two lines of the verse) that occurs through most of the poem and ask them to join in those lines as you read the poem again. Set the class up to perform the poem with one child saying the first two lines.

● Divide the class into four groups and allocate each group a verse to read in pairs with a partner in their group. Perform the poem with each group reading their verse.

Activities

● In shared writing, ask the children to look at rhyme in the poem and see if they can find a pattern. Write down the groups of rhyming words and, as a class, add further rhyming words to each group.

● In groups, ask the children to write another verse (in dialect or standard English as they wish) between verses 3 and 4, where they continue to plead with their mother to save the chicken. The children could use some of the reasons discussed earlier and start with the same two lines used for the previous verses. Encourage them to find a rhyming pattern for their lines and use rhyming dictionaries. You could provide groups of rhyming words, for example *young/fun/run* or *die/fly/pie* for the children to use at the end of their lines. Each group could then perform their extra verses to the rest of the class.

● Ask the children to write down the words used in the poem that are from Jamaican dialect and record the standard English equivalents. Read a version of the poem with these standard English alternatives, then discuss with the children how the poem loses its pattern and rhythm when standard English is substituted.

Extension/further reading

Children could think of an occasion when they pleaded with their parents for something, for example to go on a outing, to have a pet, to stay up later, to watch a television programme and so on, and write a poem about the event. Ask them to compose the first two lines, or refrain, that will begin each verse of the poem (this could be done as a class exercise) and then go on to add their own lines to the poem.

Explore further poems by Valerie Bloom, see for example her collections *Let Me Touch the Sky* (Macmillan), *Duppy Jamboree* (CUP) and *Fruits* (Macmillan).

these couple of lines are repeated at the beginning of each of the first 3 verses and reflected in last line of each verse

Chicken Dinner

Mama, don' do it, please,
Don' cook dat chicken fe dinner,
We know dat chicken from she hatch,
She is de only one in de batch
Dat de mongoose didn' catch.
Please don' cook her fe dinner.

rhyme scheme

examples of Jamaican dialect/ accent

Mama, don' do it, please,
Don' cook dat chicken fe dinner,
Yuh mean to tell mi yuh feget
Yuh promise her to we as a pet
She now even have a chance to lay yet
An yuh want to cook her fe dinner.

repetition of 'yuh' strengthens effect of child's 'attack' on Mama

slight difference in last line of each verse

Mama, don' do it, please,
Don' cook dat chicken fe dinner,
Don' give Henrietta de chop,
Ah tell yuh what, we could swop,
We will get yuh one from de shop,
If yuh promise not to cook her fe dinner.

Mama, me really glad, yuh know,
Yuh never cook Henny fe dinner,
An she glad too, ah bet.
Oh Lawd, me suddenly feel upset,
Yuh don' suppose is somebody else pet
We eating now fe dinner?

non-standard grammar

change of tone (and structure) for last verse

trick ending finishes with a question to 'Mama' (and the reader)

Valerie Bloom

End of Term

Background

This extract comes from a collection of poems, *I saw Esau*, first published in 1947 by Iona and Peter Opie. It contains a range of rhymes that have been chanted by generations of children. 'End of Term' is a traditional poem of rhyming couplets and the second part of it is used for this extract. A lady of 90 told it to the Opies in 1946 but no one knows when it was originally written. It contains references to school days and a use of language that will not be readily familiar, but the poem can be explained and made accessible to today's children and enjoyed for the same reasons of mischievous fun.

Shared reading and discussing the text

● Explain to the children that they are going to listen to a rhyming poem which used to be chanted by schoolchildren many years ago. Add that the poem was published in a book in 1947 and that many traditions have changed in school since then.

● Tell the children to listen for the rhyming words, and then read the poem to them. At the end, ask the children to identify the rhyming pattern and see if they can point out the rhyming couplets. After this, discuss the structure of the poem with the children.

● Discuss when the children think the poem was supposed to be recited, that is, on the last day of a school term. Can they point out where in the poem this can be inferred from?

● Read the poem with the children again and underline the rhyming words. Using the whiteboard, ask the children to add more suggestions of rhyming words to each group.

● Ask the children to point out words and lines that are not unfamiliar to them. Encourage them to guess the meaning, and make a table:

Original word	Meaning
Academy	School or college
Yukky	Messy, revolting
Googly	Cricketing word for a ball that unexpectedly changes direction

● Ask the children to read the poem through to themselves and then in pairs to each other. When they have had an opportunity to become confident with the language and rhyme, ask the whole class to perform the poem.

Activities

● In shared writing, ask the children to underline the nouns in the poem. Acting as scribe, make two columns on the board, labelled *Singular* and *Plural*, and write down all the nouns in the poem, with the children prompting you as to the correct column. Establish in which column words such as *tea* and *jam* should be placed and which of the nouns cannot be made plural, for example, *milk*. Discuss some of the spelling rules for making words plural, such as by adding *s* or *es* and so on, and encourage the children to add further words to the list using the correct rule.

● During shared writing, the children could write a list of all the things they dislike most at school, for example homework, tests and so on. Collect these suggestions and ask the children to write rhyming couplets, similar to the ones in 'End of Term', for example:

No more revolting school dinners,
No more shouting for the winners.

● Then ask the children to write another poem of rhyming couplets of all the things they would miss about school during the holidays, again beginning in the same way, for example *No more special friends at break*.

● Give the children copies of the poem and ask them to write down all the adjectives they can find. Then ask them to suggest as many alternative adjectives as they can for each one. Explain that they are using *synonyms*.

Extension/further reading

See also *Poems about School* compiled by Brian Moses (Hodder Wayland) and *Where Does Laughter Begin?* selected by Wes Magee (Longman).

3: 2: W17: to continue the collection of new words from reading and work in other subjects, and make use of them in reading and writing

3: 2: W18: to infer the meaning of unknown words from context and generate a range of possible meanings, e.g. for the word 'ochre' in a particular sentence, discuss which is the most likely meaning and why

End of Term

This time tomorrow, where shall I be?
  Not in this academy!

No more Latin, no more French,
  No more sitting on a hard school bench.

No more dirty bread and butter,
  No more water from the gutter.

No more maggots in the ham,
  No more yukky bread and jam.

No more milk in dirty old jugs,
  No more cabbage boiled with slugs.

No more spiders in my bath,
  Trying hard to make me laugh.

No more beetles in my tea,
  Making googly eyes at me.

No more things to bring us sorrow,
  'Cos we won't be here tomorrow.

Traditional

school or college

subject taught to most children at this time

repetition

use of apostrophe for abbreviated form of 'because'

bench was used instead of usual chairs today

rhyming couplets

milk was provided for children in jugs in those days

bathtime implies this is about a boarding school

word from cricket to mean 'changing direction'

3: 2: T4: to choose and prepare poems for performance, identifying appropriate expression, tone, volume and use of voices and other sounds

3: 2: T5: rehearse and improve performance, taking note of punctuation and meaning

3: 2: T11: to write new or extended verses for performance based on models of 'performance' and oral poetry read, e.g. rhythms, repetition

Nishnobblers

by Roald Dahl

Background

Instruction or procedural texts follow a similar structural and linguistic format. They are written in chronological order, use the imperative verb form and include temporal connectives. This text comes from *Even More Revolting Recipes* – inspired by Roald Dahl's fascination with food. Food is an important element in many of his books – Nishnobblers themselves feature in *The Giraffe and the Pelly and Me* and are one of many fantastic-sounding sweets such as Gumglotters, Blue Bubblers and Sherbet Slurpers. The recipe for Nishnobblers is set out in the standard way, with a list of ingredients and numbered steps. There is also some use of specialist language, such as *simmering* and *tempering* (although this word is explained in the text).

Shared reading and discussing the text

● Ask the children if they have ever used a recipe, or watched anyone else use a recipe. Explain that a recipe is one kind of instruction and it is arranged in the order in which it should be done. Show the children the text and explain that this is a recipe from a book called *Even More Revolting Recipes* inspired by Roald Dahl. Ask the children if they have read *The Giraffe and the Pelly and Me* and explain that Nishnobblers are referred to in that book. Now read the extract from the book underneath the title, pointing out the use of capital letters for the names of the different kinds of sweets.

● Go through the recipe and point out the use of the imperative verb, highlighting specific examples, for example *Melt, Paint*.

● Tell the children that recipes can contain specialist language and the information is usually presented in a set way. First, show the children where the instructions state MAKES 6; explain that the quantity made is often stated in recipes. Point out where the ingredients and equipment are listed. Read this list. Point out that in this case two separate lists could have been made – one for ingredients, the other for equipment. Can the children say which item

would go in an 'Ingredients' list and which in 'Equipment'? (It would be helpful to have the items available to show the class.)

● Explain that recipes often contain specialist language – here the word *tempering* has been explained. Read this explanation. Discuss the meanings of *manageable*, *indispensable* and *masterful* used in the context of this recipe. Explain that words can have different meanings in different contexts, so it is best to try and understand the meaning of a word in context.

Activities

● Give the children a copy of the recipe with the verbs omitted as a cloze procedure.

● Working in pairs, ask the children to write down the headings and subheadings they will need to use if they are going to write a recipe, for example the name of the recipe/dish, ingredients and quantities, equipment, instructions/steps for making and cooking.

● Ask the children to think about the other amazing-sounding sweets mentioned by Roald Dahl, such as Gumglotters and Blue Blubbers. Tell the children to imagine they are going to make one of these creations, and ask them to use the headings suggested above for writing their recipe. The children could make their recipe as realistic or as creative as they wish. When they have finished writing their recipe they could draw the finished sweet.

● Ask the children to write a recipe for a different purpose, such as a recipe for a good teacher. Ingredients might include a spoonful of humour, a cup of kindness and so on.

Extension/further reading

Collect a range of different recipes and ask the children in groups to compare these and discuss whether they all use the same structural and linguistic features. Look at other recipes inspired by Roald Dahl in *Revolting Recipes* and *Even More Revolting Recipes* (Red Fox). There are also numerous other recipe books including *Cakes and Cookies for Beginners* (Usborne) and *Kids' First Cookbook* (Dorling Kindersley).

3: 2: W17: to continue the collection of new words from reading and work in other subjects, and make use of them in reading and writing

3: 2: S8: other uses of capitalisation from reading, e.g. names, headings, special emphasis

3: 2: T12: to identify the different purposes of instructional texts, e.g. recipes, route-finders, timetables, instructions, plans, rules

special font for heading

quote from the book by Roald Dahl from which Nishnobblers come

names of other imaginary sweets

equipment

ingredients

numbered steps in chronological order

capital letters for names of sweets

technical term used in cooking

temporal connective

imperative verbs

adverb qualifying verb

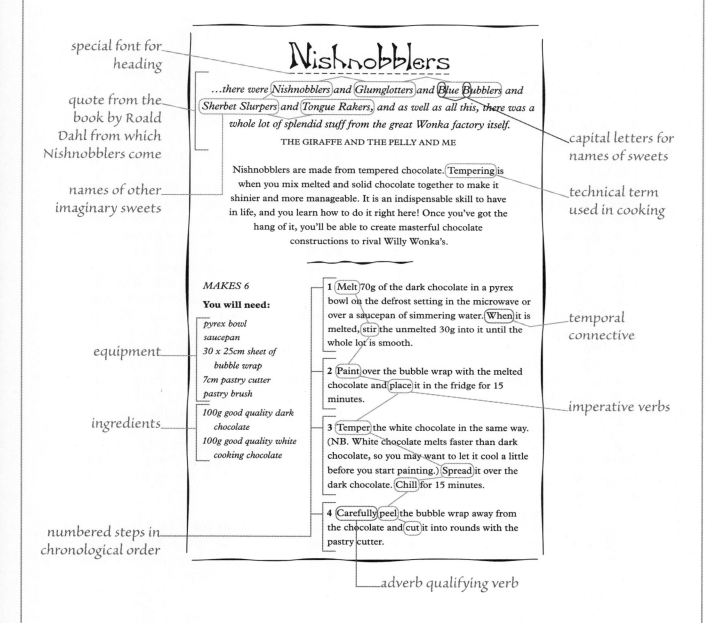

Nishnobblers

...there were Nishnobblers *and* Glumglotters *and* Blue Bubblers *and* Sherbet Slurpers *and* Tongue Rakers, *and as well as all this, there was a whole lot of splendid stuff from the great Wonka factory itself.*

THE GIRAFFE AND THE PELLY AND ME

Nishnobblers are made from tempered chocolate. Tempering is when you mix melted and solid chocolate together to make it shinier and more manageable. It is an indispensable skill to have in life, and you learn how to do it right here! Once you've got the hang of it, you'll be able to create masterful chocolate constructions to rival Willy Wonka's.

MAKES 6

You will need:

pyrex bowl
saucepan
30 x 25cm sheet of bubble wrap
7cm pastry cutter
pastry brush

100g good quality dark chocolate
100g good quality white cooking chocolate

1 Melt 70g of the dark chocolate in a pyrex bowl on the defrost setting in the microwave or over a saucepan of simmering water. When it is melted, stir the unmelted 30g into it until the whole lot is smooth.

2 Paint over the bubble wrap with the melted chocolate and place it in the fridge for 15 minutes.

3 Temper the white chocolate in the same way. (NB. White chocolate melts faster than dark chocolate, so you may want to let it cool a little before you start painting.) Spread it over the dark chocolate. Chill for 15 minutes.

4 Carefully peel the bubble wrap away from the chocolate and cut it into rounds with the pastry cutter.

3: 2: T14: how written instructions are organised, e.g. lists, numbered points, diagrams with arrows, bullet points, keys

3: 2: T15: to read and follow simple instructions

3: 2: T16: to write instructions, e.g. rules for playing games, recipes, using a range of organisational devices, e.g. lists, dashes, commas for lists in sentences, recognising the importance of correct sequence; use 'writing frames' as appropriate for support

Shrimp

Background

This second instructional text comes from a book called *Underwater Origami* devoted to 'aquatic paper folding'. The book contains instructions for making a range of sea creatures, from a starfish to a humpback whale, and even includes complicated instructions for making a diver in 37 steps! Origami is the traditional Japanese art of folding a square of paper to form a range of objects. In 1961, Samuel Randlett devised a standard system of diagrams to show how to fold the paper.

Like the recipe for 'Nishnobblers', see page 72, these instructions for making an origami shrimp are organised in chronological steps. They follow a clear numbered sequence and use diagrams.

Shared reading and discussing the text

● Tell the children that they are going to be looking at an instructional text and remind them about the different features of such texts – chronological order, imperative verbs, temporal connectives.

● Explain to the children that the instructions they are looking at come from a book called *Underwater Origami*. Give the children some background information about origami.

● Go through the instructions step by step. Start with the headings and fonts used. Then move onto exploring the chronological order and the use of numbers to help the reader. You might end with a discussion on the underwater theme and the use of specific words such as *feelers* and *antennae*.

● Read steps 4 and 5 and notice how difficult they would be to follow without diagrams.

● Ask the children to look at the diagram for step 1 and ask them if they can understand what the dotted line and arrow mean. Then read the rest of the instructions again, telling the children they will be making the shrimp for themselves later.

● Organise the children into mixed-ability pairs and tell them to read the instructions to each other and discuss the features. Ask them initially to find the imperative verbs (*fold, open, shape* and so on) and feed back to the whole class.

Activities

● In groups, give the children the instructions cut up, without the numbers, and ask them to sequence them into the correct order.

● Make sure the children have a flat surface to work on and provide small groups with squares of paper and scissors. The paper should not be too thick. Explain that you would like them to follow the instructions to step 4. At this point discuss with the children how difficult they are finding it to follow the instructions. Demonstrate how to complete step 4 if necessary. Then ask the groups to complete the task. You may need to have spare paper available to help with the less successful attempts.

● As a class, record how difficult the instructions were to follow, then ask the children if they have any ideas on how to make the instructions clearer.

● Ask the children to write instructions for their own activity, for example a game or their route to the library and so on. Remind them about the features they should include.

Extension/further reading

These instructions do not include temporal connectives. Ask more able children if they could include such words as after, when, next to see if these would improve the organisation of the procedure.

Select an activity the children have completed as a class or group, for example making a bookmark and ask the children to write instructions for this.

Further information about origami can to be found in Encarta and at the website www.britishorigami.org.uk, which will allow a range of opportunities to follow instructions.

3: 2: T14: how written instructions are organised, e.g. lists, numbered points, diagrams with arrows, bullet points, keys

3: 2: T15: to read and follow simple instructions

interesting font makes heading stand out

introductory paragraph giving information about shrimps

specialist vocabulary

sub-heading

materials needed are bulleted

instructions organised in numbered steps

imperative verbs

dotted lines indicate fold

arrow indicates direction of fold

diagrams help to explain text

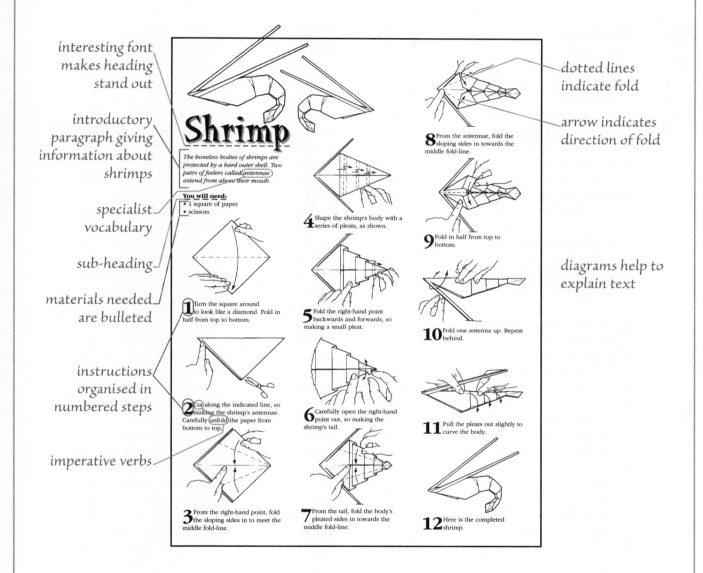

3: 2: T16: to write instructions, e.g. rules for playing games, recipes, using a range of organisational devices, e.g. lists, dashes, commas for lists in sentences, recognising the importance of correct sequence; use 'writing frames' as appropriate for support

The Witch's Tears

by Jenny Nimmo

Extract 1

Background

The atmospheric opening of *The Witch's Tears* sets the scene for this short mystery novel. A stranger comes to Theo's house to shelter from the appalling weather. Theo is convinced she is a witch who has come to steal his cat. The reader constantly questions the credibility of events, wondering if Theo has a vivid imagination or whether his instincts are correct. The only way he can be sure she is a witch is if she cries – witches' tears turn to crystal as soon as they fall. However, witches seldom cry.

Shared reading and discussing the text

● Make a list of mystery books and films the children know. Using this list, come up with a class definition of what constitutes a mystery. (For example, it may involve a strange or inexplicable situation, character or series of events. The main character will usually use clues to unravel the mystery and the reader or viewer will be kept guessing until the end.)

● Read the extract and explain that it is the opening of a mystery story. Provide an outline of the story content (see above).

● Ask the children how the author is creating an atmosphere conducive to a mystery story about a stranger who may be a witch. (The description of the weather, the gathering darkness, the birds on the wind, the dark wood, Theo's sense of urgency, his fears.)

● Collect and record the children's ideas about the relevance of the clocks and their importance to the build-up of atmosphere. The clocks tick like a heart beating, which makes the house seem as if it is alive, a safe alternative to being out in dark, stormy weather.

● Ask the children to tell you what they can about the characters of Theo and Dodie. How are they different? Which of Dodie's actions indicate that neither the weather nor the darkness bother her?

● Ask the children to find the synonyms for *said* which tell us of Theo's urgency. Encourage them to consider other synonyms which could be substituted, for example *called/shouted*.

Activities

● Tell the children they are going to create an annotated illustration to support this extract. Collect ideas from the text which they can include in their illustrations – *icy day, dark clouds tore across the sky, end of the village street, small stony cottage, dark wood behind it, flock of birds swinging on the wind* and so on. The children should draw their illustration and add on the descriptions from the text as labels.

● Discuss the use of a simile when describing the weather (*dark clouds tore across the sky like ragged horses*). Ask the children to describe other features of the weather, which could be used to create a mysterious, scary atmosphere – thunder, lightening, icicles, sharp frost, fog and so on. Encourage the children to describe these features using similes.

● Provide the children with highlighter pens and copies of the text. Ask them to highlight all the commas they can find and categorise their use (separating items in a list, in dialogue punctuation, separating a sub-clause from the main clause).

● Ask the children to write the opening of a mystery story, using descriptive language to build the atmosphere and a sense of tension. They should also describe the weather, the setting and the main character's feelings. They could include a contrast, for example the character leaving a warm, safe environment to deliver a parcel to a mysterious location such as an old manor house. Encourage them to use adjectives and similes to describe the weather and the setting.

Extension/further reading

Create a class collection of adventure and mystery stories. For example, *Harvell Angell* by Diana Hendry (Red Fox), the *Fearless Fiona* series by Karen Wallace (Young Lions). Scan through them to find other examples where a mysterious atmosphere has been created through vivid descriptions of the weather, the setting, and the characters' feelings.

3: 3: W13: to collect synonyms which will be useful in writing dialogue, e.g. *shouted, cried, yelled, squealed,* exploring the effects on meaning, e.g. through substituting these synonyms in sentences

3: 3: S7: to become aware of the use of commas in marking grammatical boundaries within sentences

3: 3: T2: to refer to significant aspects of the text, e.g. opening, build-up, atmosphere, and to know language is used to create these, e.g. use of adjectives for description

atmosphere is built up by adjectives describing the weather

simile – the clouds are compared to ragged horses

Theo's actions indicate he is afraid

further builds up threatening atmosphere

human qualities attributed to the clocks; personification

synonyms for said indicate Theo's fear and sense of urgency

The Witch's Tears

Extract 1

It was an icy day. The wind was cold enough to freeze your breath and dark clouds tore across the sky like ragged horses.

Theo, running home from school, wished that his house was closer. It stood right at the end of the village street, a small stony cottage with a dark wood behind it. They called it The Clock House, because Theo's father collected and mended clocks: old clocks with chipped feet and scratched faces that nobody wanted; clocks with pendulums, springs, wheels and tiny hammers; clocks that filled the house with a cheerful "tick-tock, tick-tock", as though its heart were beating.

"Hurry, Dodie!" Theo called to his sister who was trailing behind. She was gazing at a flock of birds, swinging on the wind like blown-about bits of cloth.

"It's getting dark," Theo shouted.

Dodie took no notice. Now she was singing to herself and pirouetting on the pavement. Dodie was seven, a red-haired, freckle-faced girl who seemed to fear nothing. Theo was older, but he was secretly afraid of the dark and found it easy to believe in ghosts. His mother said he had too much imagination. Theo couldn't help it.

commas used to mark grammatical boundaries within sentences, here to separate an adverbial clause from the main clause

the clocks are a significant aspect and contribute to the build-up of atmosphere

commas used to separate items in a list

the clocks are relevant to the plot of the story later on when they mysteriously stop

another simile – the birds are compared to blown-about bits of cloth

in contrast to Theo, Dodie's actions indicate she is carefree and not bothered by the imposing weather and impending darkness

further development of Theo's character

3: 3: T5: to discuss (i) characters' feelings; (ii) behaviour, e.g. fair or unreasonable, brave or foolish; (iii) relationships, referring to the text and making judgements

3: 3: T11: to write openings to stories or chapters linked to or arising from reading; to focus on language to create effects, e.g. building tension, suspense, creating moods, setting scenes

The Witch's Tears

by Jenny Nimmo

Extract 2

P
144

Background

The second extract from this short novel provides an ideal opportunity for studying how a character's feelings and behaviour influence the plot and help to build the atmosphere in a mystery novel. An elderly neighbour has informed Theo and Dodie that his cat has gone missing. The old man has convinced the children that witches arrive during stormy weather, on the look out for cats to steal. He has also told them that witches are hard to identify, except by their tears. Once home, in the warm, out of the storm, the tension is heightened when Theo's mother, Mrs Blossom, invites a mysterious old woman, Mrs Scarum, into the house. Theo is convinced she is a witch, wanting to steal Flora, his cat.

Shared reading and discussing the text

● Recap on the first extract and explain what happened in the following chapters using the information above. Before reading the text, ask the children to listen carefully in order to identify three things that are mysterious. (The father, uncharacteristically, has not phoned; the clocks seem to have lost their heartbeat-like rhythm; there is a stranger in the house who shows signs of being a witch – she has arrived during stormy weather and shows interest in Theo's cat.)

● Refer to the description of the clocks in the first extract – the tick-tock of the clocks was like a heart beating, the heart being the heart of the house. Ask the children what happens to the clocks in this second extract and why. (They falter at the beginning of the extract as Mrs Blossom wonders where the children's father is. At the end of the extract, it is implied that this mysterious hesitation is to do with the presence of Mrs Scarum. Theo also compares his father's heartbeat to the clocks' ticking.) Introduce the term *personification* into the discussion.

● Ask the children to discuss how Theo is feeling. He is feeling protective towards his cat and concerned that Mrs Scarum may be a witch. Encourage them to support their answers with

evidence from the text. Which dialogue words give an insight into Theo's feelings? (*Protested, sullenly, wondered, thought.*)

● Move on to talk about viewpoint. The story is written in the third person but the narrative is from Theo's point of view.

● Characters asking themselves questions helps to generate atmosphere in a mystery story. Ask the children what questions Theo asks in this extract and how they help to build the atmosphere of mystery.

Activities

● Remind the children that the story is written in the third person. Point out that it will be relatively easy to put this into the first person. In a guided writing session rewrite the incidents in this extract in the first person, from Theo's point of view. Before writing, plan what to include in the account – Theo is worried about his father; he notices the clocks have lost their rhythm; he is worried about Flora and Mrs Scarum and so on.

● Encourage the children to write a list of questions that they have about the rest of the story. They can do this in mixed-ability groups with one child chosen as the scribe. For example, they may ask: *Where is Theo's father? Is Mrs Scarum a witch? Does she want to steal Flora?* and so on. Share the questions and use them to plot the climax and resolution to the story.

Extension/further reading

The analogy between the ticking of the clocks and the beating of a heart is used throughout the novel. Make a collection of poems about time and clocks and encourage the children to read aloud or recite their favourite choices. The poems could be written up and illustrated in order to practise handwriting speed, fluency and legibility. *The Oxford Treasury of Time Poems* edited by Michael Harrison provides an excellent range of poems about time from both classic and modern poets, such as Shakespeare, Emily Dickinson and Michael Rosen.

3: 3: W13: to collect synonyms which will be useful in writing dialogue, e.g. *shouted, cried, yelled, squealed,* exploring the effects on meaning, e.g. through substituting these synonyms in sentences

3: 3: T2: to refer to significant aspects of the text, e.g. opening, build-up, atmosphere, and to know language is used to create these, e.g. use of adjectives for description

The Witch's Tears

Extract 2

personification of the clocks

names add to the characterisation of the 2 women

...Theo saw it was nearly half-past six. His father always phoned at five. He'd never missed.

"Where is he?" Mrs Blossom murmured, and as she spoke the clocks all faltered. Just for a second they lost their rhythm. Tick-creak-tock went the wooden clock. Tick-wheez-tock called the china shepherd. Tick-swish-tock mumbled the ormolu.

"Do you sleep well in a house full of ticking?" asked Mrs Scarum. "No offence. I just wondered."

"We're used to it," said Mrs Blossom. "It's comforting, especially when Mr Blossom's on his travels."

synonyms used for dialogue provide greater insight into characters' feelings

"Of course," the old woman said, and then added quickly, "My toes get so cold in winter. You'll let your little cat keep me warm tonight, won't you?"

"No! No! No!" protested Theo. "Don't let her!"

"What's got into you?" his mother complained. "Shouting like that. It's rude."

"But Flora belongs to me," said Theo, sullenly.

adverb reveals Theo is sulking

"Flora belongs to no one." Mrs Scarum leant close to him. "A cat goes where it wants to. You can't make it stay. It's got a powerful will, has a cat."

Theo was struck dumb. He looked round desperately, to see if Flora was safe. But there she was, curled in her chair and purring gently.

Mrs Blossom offered her guest a hot water bottle, but Mrs Scarum wasn't happy. "It's not the same as a cat," she grumbled.

Theo's feelings are revealed by his thoughts

If only she'd go, thought Theo. If only the blizzard would turn away and let her go back to where she came from. If only Dad were here. He turned to the shepherd clock, wishing its hands would tell him it was morning, and there was still a chance that the day would be fine, and a mysterious stranger wouldn't be forced to shelter in their home.

repetition for effect

questions help to make this a mystery story

How can I tell if our guest is a witch, wondered Theo, if witches hardly ever cry? Once again he felt the clocks hesitate, and there was a curious bend in time, a tock-ticking, un-winding of confused springs and pendulums. And he thought of his father, whose heart beat like a clock. Why hadn't he phoned? Was he caught somewhere on an icy road, or lost on the moor and slowly freezing?

simile

3: 3: T5: to discuss (i) characters' feelings; (ii) behaviour, e.g. fair or unreasonable, brave or foolish; (iii) relationships, referring to the text and making judgements

3: 3: T12: to write a first person account, e.g. write a character's own account of incident in story read

Clockwork

by Philip Pullman

Background

Philip Pullman is a master at building up suspense and atmosphere as this opening extract to his short mystery novel, *Clockwork,* demonstrates. The novel opens with the townsfolk of a small German town gathering in the tavern on the eve of the unveiling of a new figure for the town clock. It is the custom that the clockmaker's apprentice makes the clockwork figure but gradually it is revealed that all is not well…

Shared reading and discussing the text

● Read the opening paragraph with the children and ask them what kind of story they think this is. Do they have any ideas about why the writer has added *when time ran by clockwork*? You may need to ascertain that they are all clear about the meanings of *clockwork*.

● Now read the next two paragraphs. Check any unfamiliar vocabulary with the children (for example, *sauerkraut, Burgomaster*). Working in pairs, ask the children to describe the pictures the passage conjures up for them.

● Finish reading the extract and ask the children to conjecture why Karl is so miserable. What are their predictions as to the turn of events on the next day?

● Ask the children to identify – in pairs – some of the particularly powerful words Pullman uses that help create a picture of the scene for them. Note that they may pick up on both verbs and adjectives; if so, highlight these in different colours and draw the children's attention to their different functions.

● Ask the children who they think is telling the story. Who is the *I* who features in the opening paragraph? Is the story told in the first person after that?

Activities

● Highlight examples of apostrophes used for contraction and ask children to supply the omitted letters (for example, *it is, should not*). Then re-read some of the spoken sentences that include contractions but use their longer form. Ask the children why they think we use contracted forms in spoken language.

● Remind the children – or get them to remind you – about the conventions of punctuating direct speech. Focus on the final three paragraphs, which include direct speech. Split the class into three, with one group reading the Burgomaster's words, one group Herr Ringelman's and one group narrating. As the children read the spoken language, highlight the words to emphasise the positioning of the speech marks.

● Working in pairs with whiteboards, the children could go on to compose what they think the clockmaker's reply to the Burgomaster is. Tell them to focus firstly on what they think he'll say and then to concentrate on punctuating it. Can they include an apostrophe used for contraction? Share examples.

● Ask the children to rewrite the extract as a first person account, from the viewpoint of the Burgomaster or of one of the onlookers in the bar who have witnessed the arrival of Herr Ringelman and his disconsolate apprentice.

Extension

Using the passage, children could draw and annotate a picture of the bar and its immediate surroundings. How many clues can they pick up from the text to include in their pictures?

Children can seek out further examples of apostrophes used for contraction in their reading. Start a class list of these.

3: 3: W11: to use the apostrophe to spell further contracted forms, e.g. *couldn't*

3: 3: W12: to continue the collection of new words from reading and work in other subjects, and making use of them in reading and writing

3: 3: S4: to use speech marks and other dialogue punctuation appropriately in writing and to use the conventions which mark boundaries between spoken words and the rest of the sentence

double meaning – literally means the clock's mechanism, the way it works, but also about things running smoothly, regularly and automatically

typical opening phrase juxtaposed against reference to book's title – arouses reader's curiosity

chatty 1st person narrator

paragraph establishing setting

use of sight, sound and smell senses to build up atmosphere

typical German dish, made of cabbage

adjectives for description

contrast between characters

full stop inside speech marks

direct announcement of trouble to come

change of tone, narrator's 'voice'

spooky atmosphere

contrast of warm, cosy tavern with wintry night outside

fireplace

powerful verbs

younger person learning a craft from an older, experienced one

similar to a town mayor

apostrophes used for contraction

CLOCKWORK

Once upon a time (when time ran by clockwork), a strange event took place in a little German town. Actually, it was a series of events, all fitting together like the parts of a clock, and although each person saw a different part, no-one saw the whole of it; but here it is, as well as I can tell it.

It began on a winter's evening, when the townsfolk were gathering in the White Horse Tavern. The snow was blowing down from the mountains, and the wind was making the bells shift restlessly in the church tower. The windows were steamed up, the stove was blazing brightly, Putzi the old black cat was snoozing on the hearth; and the air was full of the rich smells of sausage and sauerkraut, of tobacco and beer. Gretl the little barmaid, the landlord's daughter, was hurrying to and fro with foaming mugs and steaming plates.

The door opened, and fat white flakes of snow swirled in, to faint away into water as they met the heat of the parlour. The incomers, Herr Ringelmann the clockmaker and his apprentice Karl, stamped their boots and shook the snow off their greatcoats.

"It's Herr Ringelmann!" said the Burgomaster. "Well, old friend, come and drink some beer with me! And a mug for young what's his name, your apprentice."

Karl the apprentice nodded his thanks and went to sit by himself in a corner. His expression was dark and gloomy.

"What's the matter with young thingamajig?" said the Burgomaster. "He looks as if he's swallowed a thundercloud."

"Oh, I shouldn't worry," said the old clockmaker, sitting down at the table with his friends. "He's anxious about tomorrow. His apprenticeship is coming to an end, you see."

"Ah, of course!" said the Burgomaster. It was the custom that when a clockmaker's apprentice finished his period of service, he made a new figure for the great clock of Glockenheim. "So we're to have a new piece of clockwork in the tower! Well, I look forward to seeing it tomorrow."

implication that all will not be well tomorrow

3: 3: T2: to refer to significant aspects of the text, e.g. opening, build-up, atmosphere, and to know language is used to create these, e.g. use of adjectives for description

3: 3: T11: to write openings to stories or chapters linked to or arising from reading; to focus on language to create effects, e.g. building tension, suspense, creating moods, setting scenes

3: 3: T3: to distinguish between 1st and 3rd person accounts

3: 3: T12: to write a first person account, e.g. write a character's own account of incident in story read

Rosie's Zoo

by Ailie Busby

Background

This is an extract from a picture book for slightly younger children, which follows the adventures of Rosie as she goes in search of animals for her zoo. Although the text provides an easier read for Year 3, it is a useful extract on which to base extended story writing, rather than solely for reading comprehension. It provides a clear adventure-story structure which Year 3 children can identify and utilise; use of different settings; adjectives to describe humorous characters and fantasy foods; a repeated dialogue pattern; time phrases and strong verb choices.

Shared reading and discussing the text

● Read the extract to the children and establish the story structure: 1. Rosie has a problem – she wants to play zoo but she has no animals; 2. To solve her problem she sets off on a journey to find some – in a rocket; 3. She goes to one destination – the moon; 4. She finds an elephant – small and green; 5. He bargains with her for food – juicy pumpkins; 6. She agrees and promises the juiciest pumpkins ever tasted. This pattern is repeated throughout the book until Rosie has enough animals to play zoo. The story features different locations and different modes of transport and Rosie meets unusual animals who all request strange food.

● Provide the children with a copy of the extract and ask them to highlight the description of Rosie's journey to the moon and her landing. Discuss the choice of adjectives and verbs, for example *tallest*; *very dark*; *glittery*; *big, round* and *whooshing, landed*. Ask the children to identify any time phrases used to sequence the story (*after hours and hours and a few minutes for luck…*) and any fantasy story features (green elephants on the moon).

● Ask the children to highlight the dialogue between Rosie and the animals she meets. A question is followed with a question, which Rosie answers with a promise. Tell them that this dialogue structure is repeated throughout the book.

Activities

● In shared writing, tell the children they are going to plan a picture story for younger children (possibly for Reception or Year 1 children at the school, thus providing them with a real incentive and audience) based on *Rosie's Zoo*. Remind them of the story structure as mapped out above. Put the children in pairs and ask them to suggest alternatives for: modes of transport (such as a submarine, a hand-glider, a steam train, a go-cart, a skate board and so on); destinations (for example, deep under the sea, a rainforest, a cave); animals (a purple pig in a woolly bobble hat); food requests (chips with strawberry jam). You may like to record suggestions from the whole class into a table on the board. Choose one destination, transport mode, animal and food request and together plan the next chapter of the story. Ask the children to help you brainstorm ideas for phrases to describe the journey and how long it takes.

● Ask the children to write their own version of *Rosie's Zoo* – calling it by their own name and changing zoo to safari park, farm, water-life park and so on, such as *Javed's Farm*. Provide a story planning sheet and encourage careful use of verbs and adjectives. Remind them of the dialogue structure used in the story. On completion of the sheets, the children can draft and write up their stories. Provide less able children with an outline story written in the style of a cloze passage where the descriptions of the animals, transport, the journey and so on are omitted, allowing them to make their own choices but providing a sentence structure.

Extension/further reading

There are several picture book adventure stories which provide a clear model for younger children's story writing, including *A Busy Day for a Good Grandmother* by Margaret Mahy (Puffin Books), *The Mousehole Cat* by Antonia Barber (Walker Books) and *Mrs Armitage on Wheels* by Quentin Blake (Red Fox).

3: 3: S4: to use speech marks and other dialogue punctuation appropriately in writing and to use the conventions which mark boundaries between spoken words and the rest of the sentence

3: 3: S6: to investigate through reading and writing how words and phrases can signal time sequences, e.g. *first, then, after, meanwhile, from, where*

Rosie's Zoo

3rd person account

problem established at beginning

adjectives describe journey

signals passing of time

dialogue pattern repeated at each stage of story

superlative adjective

"I want to play zoo," said Rosie.
She looked around her room. She had lots of toys, in fact, she had hundreds, but as she looked closer she couldn't see any of her favourite animals.
"This is terrible. How can I play zoo if I can't find my animals?" said Rosie out loud.
Something red shone brightly from the corner of the room and caught her eye... her space rocket!
"I know," said Rosie, "I will go to the moon, the only sensible place to find missing toys," she said.
"Up, up and away," cried Rosie and she took off.

Whooshing up through the sky, past houses, past trees, past the tallest buildings, until suddenly it was very dark indeed. Only the twinkle of the glittery stars and the big, round moon broke the darkness.

After hours and hours and a few minutes for luck, the rocket landed on the moon with a bumpety-bump. In the distance, Rosie could see four elephants walking in a line. As they came closer, she noticed that one of the elephants was small and green.

"Would you like to be in my zoo?" she asked politely.
"Will we eat juicy pumpkins?" asked the elephant.
"The juiciest pumpkins you've ever tasted," said Rosie. So the little green elephant said goodbye to his friends and climbed on board Rosie's rocket. Whoosh! Off they went to find more animals.

simple story structure provides clear, repetitive format:

mode of transport

destination

meets animal

food request

brings this section of story to a close

3: 3: T1: to re-tell main points of story in sequence

3: 3: T10: to plot a sequence of episodes modelled on a known story, as a plan for writing

3: 3: T13: to write more extended stories based on a plan of incidents and set out in simple chapters with titles and author details; to use paragraphs to organise the narrative

Horse Pie

by Dick King-Smith

Background

Dick King-Smith is a well-known children's author who has had a varied career, including 20 years as a farmer, serving as a lieutenant in the Grenadier Guards during World War II and working as a primary school teacher. His great love of animals makes them the focus of most of his writing. His work provides a wide range of texts suitable for comparison and contrast in Year 3. Three extracts have been chosen to cover the range *stories by the same author*. In *Horse Pie*, snobbery, pride and prejudice are all overcome when, Jenny, an old seaside donkey, comes to live in a home for retired horses and saves the lives of three giant horses. In this extract, the opening of the book, we meet Jenny and read dialogue between her owner and his son as they discuss her fate. The reader's heart immediately goes out to Jenny, hoping that a new home will be found for her where she can retire happily.

Shared reading and discussing the text

● Ask the children who has heard of Dick King-Smith and if they have read any of his books. Make a list of titles suggested and ask the children to recall each book's main character and theme. Ask them to express their opinions and preferences. Tell the children about Dick King-Smith. It would also be useful to collect and display a range of his books. Explain that you are going to compare and contrast three different extracts by Dick King-Smith. Following this, the children will vote for which of the three books they would choose to read, giving reasons for their choice.

● Read the extract with the children and point out how it opens with a bold statement (*'She'll have to go'*), which leads into dialogue about the fate of Jenny. Ask the children why Jenny has to go and what options are open for her. Sum up what the opening passage achieves – it endears us towards Jenny, makes us feel sorry for her and adds drama, causing us to want to find out what happens to her.

● Discuss Sam's behaviour – what does he do

that shows he is thinking carefully about what his father is suggesting? (He squiggles sand between his toes). What does Sam do to save Jenny? (He writes to the Old Horses' Home to see if they will take her.)

● Sam writes a persuasive letter to the Old Horses' Home (*'Pulls at your heart-strings, doesn't it, boss?'*). We don't hear the whole letter – only the key persuasive words such as *her last hope, Please, please!* Ask the children to suggest what else Sam would have included in his letter. List their suggestions on the board and encourage them to select vocabulary and style appropriate to the intended reader.

● Ask the children to highlight all the pronouns and nouns which refer to Jenny (*She, Jenny, the old girl, her*). Distinguish between personal and possessive pronouns, third person pronouns and proper nouns. Discuss how pronouns are used to mark gender and notice how in speech and reading they stand in place of nouns.

● Ask the children to highlight the punctuation used in some of the dialogue in the extract. Focus on the conventions used to mark the boundaries between the spoken words and the rest of the sentence.

Activities

● The children could write their own persuasive letter as if they were Sam – prompt them to include why Jenny deserves to retire happily, how hard she has worked and what will become of her if the Home can't take her. Provide less able children with a selection of sentences, which they could sequence to form their own version of the letter.

● Point out the use of the word *pleaded* as a synonym for *said* and how it conveys Sam's reactions to his dad's comments. Ask the children to highlight where *said* is used in the extract and replace each one with a different dialogue word (or add on adverbs to say how the words were spoken). For less able children, provide a list of synonyms from which they can choose, for example *stated, asked, explained, sighed, shouted* and *agreed*.

3: 3: W11: to use the apostrophe to spell further contracted forms, e.g. *couldn't*

3: 3: W13: to collect synonyms which will be useful in writing dialogue, e.g. *shouted, cried, yelled, squealed,* exploring the effects on meaning, e.g. through substituting these synonyms in sentences

3: 3: S2: to identify pronouns and understand their functions in sentences

3: 3: S4: to use speech marks and other dialogue punctuation appropriately in writing and to use the conventions which mark boundaries between spoken words and the rest of the sentence

opens with a bold statement

conventions of dialogue punctuation

comma used to mark sub-clause

shocking phrase – how does this link to the title?

2 short, dramatic conversations tell a lot of story

description of donkey's new home indicates it is a pleasant place

synonym for 'said', conveys how Sam is feeling

different nouns and pronouns all refer to Jenny

change of time and place

persuasive language

apostrophe used to spell contracted forms

story given a hook – who are these giants?

Horse Pie

"She'll have to go," said the donkeyman.

"Who?" said his son, Sam.

"Old Jenny. She's got so slow. Didn't you see that kid just now trying to make her walk a bit faster? She was miles behind the others. She's past it."

Sam squiggled sand between his bare toes as he looked at the line of donkeys waiting patiently for their next riders.

"What will happen to her, Dad?" he said.

"Have to see if they've got room at the Donkey Sanctuary," said his father.

"And if they haven't?"

"Cat's meat, I'm afraid," said the donkeyman.

"You mean…?"

"Yes. Have to send the old girl to the slaughterhouse."

"Oh, Dad, you couldn't! Not old Jenny!" Sam pleaded.

"Well, you think of a better idea then."

"Have a look at this," said the Manager of the Old Horses' Home to his stableman, a couple of days later.

"What is it, boss?"

"Letter from a kid. Son of the chap that keeps the beach donkeys at Easton-super-Mare."

The stableman read the letter.

" '…Donkey Sanctuary full up… slaughterhouse… you are her last hope… Please, please!' Oh dear, pulls at your heart-strings doesn't it, boss?"

The Manager nodded.

"He can't bear to think of her going to the knackers. We can make room for her, can't we?"

"Sure, boss," said the stableman. "What's one more among so many?"

And indeed there were a great many animals in the large, tree-shaded field in front of the Old Horses' Home. They were of all shapes and sizes, and all possible colours, and most of them were well past their prime. But amongst all the ancient ponies and horses were three giants who were in fact, not old.

3: 3: S7: to become aware of the use of commas in marking grammatical boundaries within sentences

3: 3: T2: to refer to significant aspects of the text, e.g. opening

3: 3: T5: to discuss characters' feelings

3: 3: T8: to compare and contrast works by the same author, e.g. different stories, stories sharing similar themes

The Guard-Dog

by Dick King-Smith

Background

This extract is from another story by Dick King-Smith with a similar theme to *Horse Pie*, in that the main character (an animal evoking sympathy with the reader) is faced with life in a home. The story begins earlier in a pet shop, where the scruffy little mongrel is laughed at by other pedigree dogs because he wants to be a guard-dog. He is eventually bought, but due to an ear-splitting bark is soon sent to a Dog's Home, where potential owners are attracted to him and consider taking him home until he begins to bark. Our extract begins after new owners have chosen most of the intakes but the guard-dog has sadly been left behind. The extract is also rich in material for inference and deduction.

Shared reading and discussing the text

● Ask the children to recount the previous extract, *Horse Pie* – highlighting that it was an animal story in which the main character was a sad, old donkey who was of no use any more and needed to find a loving home in order to be saved from certain death. Hold a discussion about unwanted pets and the role of organisations such as the RSPCA and Battersea Dogs' Home to establish background knowledge. Read the extract from *The Guard-Dog* with the children and ask them to compare it with the previous extract, listing their suggestions for similarities and differences on the board. Encourage them to identify the theme behind the two extracts.

● Ask the children to build a character portrait of the guard-dog's neighbour – the terrier (he is old, rather smelly, very sad, grumpy, resigned to his fate, reluctant to talk, wants to be left alone and speaks with a non-standard English dialect). Ask the children to explain what is going to happen to the terrier (he is going to be destroyed) and to find in the text examples which show how he feels about this.

● Time phrases are very important in the context of the extract: fourteen days is the time limit for a dog's stay in the home. Ask the children to highlight any words or phrases which relate to time in the text. Encourage them to infer why the opening phrase, *By the thirteenth day,* is so important to the guard-dog (the next day could be his last).

Activities

● Point out to the children that the extract is written in the third person. Discuss how the guard-dog feels about being in the Dogs' Home; how he doesn't understand what will happen to the old terrier; and how he may feel when he realises what becomes of dogs on their fourteenth day at the Home. Put key words on the board such as *lonely* and *frightened* and ask them to write the guard-dog's own account of the incidents in the story.

● Examine the terrier's dialect with the children, drawing attention to the non-standard spelling and grammar. In shared writing, put the terrier's dialect into standard English, using corrected spellings and ensuring grammatical agreement of pronouns and verbs.

● Tell the children they are going to write the opening to the next chapter. Provide them with the opening sentence, *It was the beginning of the guard-dog's fourteenth day in the Dogs' Home.* Discuss with the children what might happen and give them the choice of writing in either the first or third person. Less able children could work as a group with you or an LSA taking the role of scribe.

● Having read two pieces by the same author, the children could write a comparative review detailing who the main characters are, the themes of the stories, how they would like the stories to end and which book they would choose to read. Less able children could be given an outline review for completion.

Extension/further reading

Another short story about animals by Dick King-Smith where the main character has a dream of a new life is *All Because of Jackson* (Corgi), the tale of an unusual rabbit who dreams of going to sea on a tall sailing ship.

3: 3: S1: to use awareness of grammar to decipher new or unfamiliar words

3: 3: S3: to ensure grammatical agreement in speech and writing of pronouns and verbs, e.g. *I am, we are*, in standard English

3: 3: S4: to use speech marks and other dialogue punctuation appropriately in writing and to use the conventions which mark boundaries between spoken words and the rest of the sentence

The Guard-Dog

By the thirteenth day, there was only one dog left of those who had been there when he was admitted. This was his next-door neighbour, an old and rather smelly terrier.

The guard-dog's attempts to make conversation with it had always thus far been met with a surly growl, so he was quite surprised when he was suddenly addressed.

"You bin in 'ere thirteen days, littl'un, an't you?" said the terrier.

"Oh," said the guard-dog, "have I?"

"Ar. You come in day after I. 'Tis my fourteenth day."

"Oh well," said the guard-dog, "try not to worry. I'm sure you'll soon be gone."

"Ar," said the terrier. "I shall. Today."

"But how can you know that? How can you know that someone's going to take you away today?"

"Fourteen days is the limit, littl'un. They don't keep you no longer than that."

"Why, what do they do with you then?"

"An't nobody told you?"

"No."

"Ar well," said the old terrier. "'Tis all right for us old uns, 'tis time to go. I shan't be sorry. You don't feel nothing, they do say. But 'tis a shame for a nipper like you."

"I don't understand," said the guard-dog. "What are you trying to tell me?" But though he kept on asking, the old dog only growled at him, and then lay silent, staring blankly out of its kennel. Later, a man in a white coat came and led it gently away.

phrase signals passing of time

dialogue punctuation conventions

terrier is going to be put down – although this isn't stated, it can be inferred

guard-dog's innocence endears us to him even more; we want to read on to see what happens to him

time connective

2 sentences are joined by conjunction 'so'

non-standard English: builds terrier's character

behaviour of terrier indicates he is resigned to his fate and no longer wishes to be disturbed

3: 3: S5: how sentences can be joined in more complex ways through using a widening range of conjunctions in addition to *'and'* and *'then,'* e.g. *if, so*

3: 3: S6: to investigate through reading and writing how words and phrases can signal time sequences, e.g. *first, then*

3: 3: T8: to compare and contrast works by the same author, e.g. different stories, stories sharing similar themes

3: 3: T9: to be aware of authors and to discuss preferences and reasons for these

The Finger-Eater

by Dick King-Smith

Background

The third extract by Dick King-Smith has been chosen to provide a contrast with the other two. Written in the style of a traditional tale, this story is gruesome, funny and based around a rather unusual troll with a nasty habit, as opposed to an animal with whom the reader takes pity. The extract enables children to see that Dick King-Smith does write stories around subject matters other than animals. When dealing with this text is it important to focus on the fact that Ulf is considered gruesome because of his bad habit – eating people's fingers and *not* because of his appearance. Dick King-Smith has written this story in the style of a traditional fairy tale where the bad are portrayed as ugly and the good are beautiful. Children tend to love this gruesome little character and find him quite endearing, despite the fact that he is a mischievous 'baddy'. It may be useful to look at the portrayal of Ulf with your class as a PSHE discussion point in order to ensure that the children don't make stereotypes where beauty equals good and anything less is bad.

Shared reading and discussing the text

● Ask the children to recap on what they have learnt about Dick King-Smith as an author so far. Explain that this third extract is based on a different subject and that they will be contrasting it with the previous two.

● Read the extract and elicit from the children that it is written in the style of a traditional tale, for example the use of the phrase *long long ago* and a troll who is very bad. Then ask them to retell the main points in sequence.

● Ask the children to contrast the story with the previous two extracts by Dick King-Smith. Encourage the children to draw similarities between this story and traditional tales such as 'The Three Billy Goats Gruff'.

● Ask the children to consider the credibility of events – this story is completely imaginary whereas the previous two extracts are based on real animals in likely situations (although in reality the animals would not speak!). Ulf is an

entirely fictitious character.

● Ask the children to highlight all the nouns and pronouns associated with the troll and to distinguish them according to type.

Activities

● Discuss with the children what they think will happen in the story. Do they think that Ulf will be punished for his behaviour? Will the people who lost their fingers get revenge? Ask them how the resolution may differ from the previous extracts – there the reader hoped for happy endings for Jenny and the guard-dog. Provide the children with a blank storyboard with space for about eight drawings and one or two sentences under each drawing. Ask them to plot the story as detailed so far in the extract and then bring the story to a climax and resolution. (In Dick King-Smith's story, Ulf is tricked by a clever little girl and loses his teeth so he is no longer able to bite off fingers. He disappears down a hole in a sulk and is never seen again!)

● Explain that this story is written in the style of a traditional fairy story where the characters are easily identified as 'good' and 'wicked'. Provide the children with a selection of fairy tale picture books and ask them to identify other characters who are portrayed as 'wicked'. Ask the children to list the characters and detail what it is that makes them bad. Focus on the *behaviour* of the wicked character. If the children associate the 'baddy' with physical appearances, point out that in 'Goldilocks and the Three Bears', Goldilocks, who is the 'baddy', is actually a pretty little girl.

● Having studied three extracts by Dick King-Smith, provide the children with a card on which they write the name of the book they would like to read and the reason why. Ask each child to read aloud his/her card. Hold a ballot to see which extract was the most popular. As the three books are fairly short, they could all be read to the class. Children could also design posters or write blurbs about their favourite Dick King-Smith book.

3: 3: W9: to recognise and spell prefixes

3: 3: S2: to identify pronouns and understand their functions in sentences

3: 3: S6: to investigate through reading and writing how words and phrases can signal time sequences, e.g. *first, then, after, meanwhile, from, where*

3: 3: T2: to refer to significant aspects of the text, e.g. opening, build-up, atmosphere, and to know language is used to create these, e.g. use of adjectives for description

opening contains traditional-tale elements

prefix gives clue to meaning

fictitious, traditional-tale characters

pronouns relating to the main character:

proper noun

3rd person form of pronoun

important use of adverb indicating how troll speaks; this is the opposite of how we would imagine a troll to speak

common noun

The Finger-Eater

Long long ago, in the cold lands of the North, there lived a most unusual troll.

Like all the hill-folk (so called because they usually made their homes in holes in the hills) he was hump-backed and bow-legged, with a frog-face and bat-ears and razor-sharp teeth.

But he grew up (though, like all other trolls, not very tall) with an extremely bad habit –

he liked to eat fingers!

Ulf (for that was his name) always went about this in the same way. Whenever he spied someone walking alone on the hills, he would come up, smiling broadly, and hold out a hand, and say politely:

"How do you do?"

Now trolls are usually rude and extremely grumpy and don't care how anyone does, so the person would be pleasantly surprised at meeting such a jolly one, and would hold out his or her hand to shake Ulf's.

Then Ulf would take it and, quick as a flash, bite off a finger with his razor-sharp teeth and run away as fast as his bow-legs would carry him, chewing like mad and grinning all over his frog-face.

Strangers visiting those parts were amazed to see how many men, women and children were lacking a finger on their right hands, especially children, because their fingers were more tender and much sought after by Ulf.

Nobody lacked more than one finger, because even small children weren't foolish enough to shake hands if they met Ulf a second time, but ran away with them deep in their pockets.

dramatic pause, increases tension

time connectives

conjunction joins sentences

possessive pronoun

personal pronoun

description of behaviour reveals a lot about character

3: 3: T4: to consider credibility of events

3: 3: T5: to discuss (i) characters' feelings; (ii) behaviour, e.g. fair or unreasonable, brave or foolish

3: 3: T8: to compare and contrast works by the same author, e.g. different stories, sequels using same characters in new settings, stories sharing similar themes

Monday's Child...

by Colin McNaughton and traditional

Poems 1 and 2

Background

Colin McNaughton's 'Monday's Child is Red and Spotty' is a contemporary take on the well-known traditional rhyme, which claims to predict what a child's character will be like based on the day of the week on which they were born. McNaughton is a humorous and lively author-illustrator and his typically anarchic approach to poetry will appeal to children of this age. Whilst both poem structures are the same, the contemporary version is humorous – no matter which day the child is born on, he/she is bound to have mischievous traits. The traditional version will require discussion, as it will contain unfamiliar vocabulary. The modern version, on the other hand, will have instant appeal for children, with its simple vocabulary and easy rhyming couplets.

Shared reading and discussing the text

● Discuss what is meant by *superstition* and *superstitious sayings* and encourage the children to give examples of any they have heard. For example, *Red sky at night, shepherd's delight.*

● Ask the children if they know which day of the week they were born on. Explain that there is a traditional poem, which supposedly tells a parent what their child's personality will be like, according to the day on which they were born.

● Read the traditional version of the poem first. There will be unfamiliar vocabulary within the poem which will require explanation – provide the children with dictionaries to look up meanings. Anticipate comments on *gay.* Reinforce the fact that the poem is based only on superstition and that people cannot be categorised into seven personality traits. Use this opportunity to discuss other characteristics, for example shy, brave, timid, foolish.

● Explain that a modern, humorous version of the poem has been written using the same format. Read the poem to the children and ask for their reactions. What makes the poem funny?

● Look at the use of the apostrophe for the days: Monday*'*s child is the child born on a Monday or belonging to Monday. Contrast this with the apostrophe for contraction in *won't.*

Activities

● Use the poem to practise spelling the days of the week. The poems could be word-processed and displayed in the class or used as a handwriting exercise.

● Ask pairs of children to read through both poems to identify the rhyming pairs of lines – there are four pairs in each poem. Three of these pairs contain words that have long vowel phonemes sounding the same but spelt differently. Ask the children to identify the vowel sound and explain how it is spelt in each case. Ask them to think of other words that have these vowel sounds and categorise them according to spelling.

● Using rhyming dictionaries and the work carried out on vowel phonemes, build up a pool of rhyming words which the children can use to write their own version of the poem (*nappy/happy, sleep/deep, room/doom, habit/rabbit* and so on). Discuss the structure of the poem with the children: it has eight lines of four rhyming couplets; the first six lines begin with the days of the week up to Saturday and all have capital letters. For less able children, provide them with the structure of the poem written out with gaps for them to insert rhyming words. The rhyming words could be provided on cards for them to read and pair up. The children could recite their finished poems.

Extension/further reading

The anthologies *The Hippo Book of Silly Poems* compiled by John Foster and *The Day I Fell Down the Toilet and Other Poems* by Steve Turner (Lion Publishing) provide a large selection of humorous poms which will have strong appeal for seven and eight year-olds. Children could select favourites to be written up and compiled into a class anthology. See *There's an Awful Lot of Weirdos in Our Neighbourhood* (Walker Books) for more humorous Colin McNaughton poems.

3: 3: W1: the spelling of words containing each of the long vowel phonemes from KS1 (Appendix List 3)

3: 3: W2: to:
● identify phonemes in speech and writing
● blend phonemes for reading
● segment words into phonemes for spelling

traditional version of poem is used to predict what a child will be like if born on a certain day of the week

attractive

elegant/polite

sad

traditional version contains unfamiliar vocabulary

Monday's child...

Monday's child is fair of **face;** [A]
Tuesday's child is full of **grace;** [A]
Wednesday's child is full of **woe;** [B]
Thursday's child has far to **go;** [B]
Friday's child is loving and **giving;** [C]
Saturday's child works hard for a **living;** [C]
The child that is born on the Sabbath **day,** [D]
Is <u>bonny</u>, and <u>blithe</u>, and good, and **gay.** [D]

Traditional

regular rhyme structure

rhyming couplets

will be successful

happy and full of fun

carefree

healthy-looking, happy

humorous version conjures up images of a naughty toddler

apostrophe used to show possession

apostrophe used to spell contracted forms

Monday's Child is Red and Spotty

Monday's child is red and **spotty,** [A]
Tuesday's child won't use the **potty.** [A]
Wednesday's child won't go to **bed,** [B]
Thursday's child will not be **fed.** [B]
Friday's child breaks all the **toys,** [C]
Saturday's child makes all the **noise.** [C]
And the child that's born on the seventh **day** [D]
Is a pain in the neck like the rest, **OK!** [D]

Colin McNaughton

regular rhyme structure

rhyming couplets

vowel phoneme sounds the same but is spelt differently: t<u>oy</u>s/ n<u>oi</u>se

this version easier to understand from child's point of view as vocabulary is more familiar

3: 3: W3: to read and spell correctly the high frequency words from KS1 (Appendix List 1)

3: 3: T6: to compare forms or types of humour, e.g. by exploring, collecting and categorising form or type of humour, e.g. word play, joke poems, word games, absurdities, cautionary tales, nonsense verse, calligrams

3: 3: T7: to select, prepare, read aloud and recite by heart poetry that plays with language or entertains; to recognise rhyme, alliteration and other patterns of sound that create effects

The Ceremonial Band

by James Reeves

Background

This poem has been specifically written to be performed out loud by a chorus and several solo voices. It plays with patterns of sound and has a repetitive structure, which is built on with each new verse, making it suitable for recital by heart.

Children should be encouraged to read poetry aloud and use their voices effectively. Discussion of the poem will help them to use appropriate emphasis, pause at the correct points, incorporate sound effects, and so on. They will enjoy bringing the poem to life using instruments, props and costumes. Once the poetry recital has been rehearsed, the children should be given the opportunity to perform it in front of an audience and/or record it on tape or video. Positive self-assessment and evaluation is a useful tool for building confidence and improving subsequent work.

Shared reading and discussing the text

● Before providing the children with a copy of the poem, explain that you are going to read a performance poem, which uses onomatopoeia to create effect. Recite the poem and then ask the children to identify any patterns. They may notice repeated lines and an extra instrument in each verse as well as made-up words for the sounds of the instruments.

● If possible, show the children (pictures of) each instrument and let them hear what it sounds like. If this is not possible, describe each instrument and the sound it makes. Discuss the choice of words in the poem to represent the sounds made by the instruments.

Activities

● Hand out copies of the poem to pairs of children and ask them to:
- Number the verses.
- Highlight in one colour the repeated lines in each verse (lines 1–3 and the last line).

- Highlight the sounds made by the instruments in another colour.
- Highlight the names of the instruments in a third colour.

Discuss the structure of the poem – there are five verses, each containing four repeated lines, the first verse contains two instruments which 'speak' and each subsequent verse has an additional instrument built into it. The last line of the last verse is repeated for effect.

● Discuss how the poem could be performed – the repeated lines could be recited by the whole class with individual children taking on the role of each instrument and a small group reciting the rest (*said the drum*, *said the flute* and so on). Practise performing the poem and experimenting with the way in which the instruments say their sounds.

● *Said* is used throughout the poem. Explain that *said* could be replaced with synonyms to reflect the way in which each instrument spoke. For example, replace *said* with *sang* for the flute and *boomed* for the bass. Encourage the children to use a thesaurus to come up with suggestions. Remind them that these new words can only be made up of one syllable to maintain the rhythm of the poem.

Extension/further reading

Put the children into small groups and provide a collection of poetry anthologies which contain performance poems that use rhyme, alliteration and other patterns of sound to create effects, for example *Noisy Poems* collected by Jill Bennett (OUP) and pages 401–17 of *The Works* chosen by Paul Cookson (Macmillan Children's Books). Give the children a set amount of time to choose a poem to perform. Once these have been approved, give them a further set amount of time to decide how they are going to perform the poem, to learn it and rehearse it. The children can then perform the poem in front of the class.

3: 3: **W13:** to collect synonyms which will be useful in writing dialogue, e.g. *shouted, cried, yelled, squealed,* exploring the effects on meaning, e.g. through substituting these synonyms in sentences

3: 3: **W14:** to explore homonyms which have the same spelling but multiple meanings and explain how the meanings can be distinguished in context, e.g. *form* (shape or document), *wave* (gesture, shape or motion)

1st three lines repeated in each verse

speech marks punctuate the sound of each instrument

last line repeated in each verse

a small, shrill flute

instruments 'speak'

homonym (a violin/to swindle)

superlative

onomatopoeia

last line is repeated again for effect in the last verse ('For' is changed to 'Oh!')

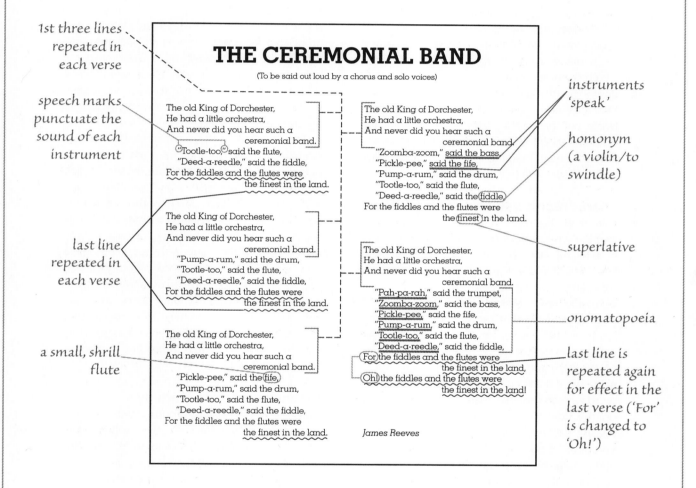

THE CEREMONIAL BAND

(To be said out loud by a chorus and solo voices)

The old King of Dorchester,
He had a little orchestra,
And never did you hear such a
　　　　　ceremonial band.
"Tootle-too," said the flute,
"Deed-a-reedle," said the fiddle,
For the fiddles and the flutes were
　　　　　the finest in the land.

The old King of Dorchester,
He had a little orchestra,
And never did you hear such a
　　　　　ceremonial band.
"Pump-a-rum," said the drum,
"Tootle-too," said the flute,
"Deed-a-reedle," said the fiddle,
For the fiddles and the flutes were
　　　　　the finest in the land.

The old King of Dorchester,
He had a little orchestra,
And never did you hear such a
　　　　　ceremonial band.
"Pickle-pee," said the fife,
"Pump-a-rum," said the drum,
"Tootle-too," said the flute,
"Deed-a-reedle," said the fiddle,
For the fiddles and the flutes were
　　　　　the finest in the land.

The old King of Dorchester,
He had a little orchestra,
And never did you hear such a
　　　　　ceremonial band.
"Zoomba-zoom," said the bass,
"Pickle-pee," said the fife,
"Pump-a-rum," said the drum,
"Tootle-too," said the flute,
"Deed-a-reedle," said the fiddle,
For the fiddles and the flutes were
　　　　　the finest in the land.

The old King of Dorchester,
He had a little orchestra,
And never did you hear such a
　　　　　ceremonial band.
"Pah-pa-rah," said the trumpet,
"Zoomba-zoom," said the bass,
"Pickle-pee," said the fife,
"Pump-a-rum," said the drum,
"Tootle-too," said the flute,
"Deed-a-reedle," said the fiddle,
For the fiddles and the flutes were
　　　　　the finest in the land,
Oh! the fiddles and the flutes were
　　　　　the finest in the land!

James Reeves

3: 3: **S4:** to use speech marks and other dialogue punctuation appropriately in writing and to use the conventions which mark boundaries between spoken words and the rest of the sentence

3: 3: **T7:** to select, prepare, read aloud and recite by heart poetry that plays with language or entertains; to recognise rhyme, alliteration and other patterns of sound that create effects

Kennings

by Steve Turner and Coral Rumble
Poems 1 and 2

Background

These two poems play with language. They are made of a series of kennings (see also page 24) – a description of a person or thing, which does not use its name. Each kenning is usually made up of two words (a noun and a noun made from a verb, using the *er* suffix) which together make up a compound noun, describing the subject through what it does. Kennings originated in Anglo-Saxon and Old Norse poetry. As they hear each kenning, the children will enjoy identifying the subject of the poem. A poem made up of a series of kennings is similar to a riddle or word puzzle.

Shared reading and discussing the text

● Remind the children of what kennings are and the work they did in Term 1 (see page 24). Give examples such as the Anglo-Saxons using kennings to name their swords or their ships, for example *throat slasher, oar steed*.

● Provide the children with copies of the poems, ensuring that they cannot see the title 'Sun' or the answer to 'Guess Who?'. Read each poem to the children and encourage them to guess the subject of the poem.

● Brainstorm what the Sun does, making a word web on the board. Display the poem 'Sun' on the board and encourage the children to analyse each kenning in turn, for example, the Sun gives us heat and light, hence *Lightbringer* and *Heatgiver*. Write an explanation of each kenning alongside the poem. Discuss the structure of 'Sun'. It is made up of 16 kennings, each kenning constituting a line (made up of two words put together to make one new word), and there are four, four-line stanzas.

● Display 'Guess Who?' on the board. Can the children use their knowledge of the Tudors to guess who it is? If the children haven't yet studied the Tudors in history, this is a good opportunity to introduce Henry VIII. Go through any unfamiliar words with the children. Draw their attention to the use of alliteration in the poem, for example *dandy dresser* as well as the rhythm of the poem. Comment also on the

layout of the poem – it is a list of 20 kennings and not punctuated until the last line.

Activities

● Ask the children to look at 'Guess Who?' and group the kennings accordingly, for example *horse rider, joust glider, music maker, tennis prancer* and *dandy dresser* tell us what Henry VIII enjoyed doing in his spare time. Other categories could include his role as king and his reputation as husband.

● Choose a relevant topic or subject for a class poem according to what the class is studying in other areas of the curriculum, or simply pick a subject, for example a mouse. Brainstorm a list of words that describe the subject or what it does – eats cheese, scuttles around at night, lives in a hole, twitches its nose and so on. Encourage the children to turn these ideas into kennings – *cheese nibbler, nose twitcher, hole dweller* and so on. Encourage the use of alliteration where appropriate. Once you have collected a suitable number, allow the children to group them and put them into stanzas. They can then go on to write out their kenning poem and illustrate it.

Extension/further reading

Provide mixed-ability groups with a bag containing a number of cards with topics or subjects suitable for kenning poems (for example, a cat, a volcano, a train, a holiday). Tell them to pick a card, assign one child as the scribe and on a large piece of paper, brainstorm their subject. They can then create kennings and collate them into a poem. When they have drafted and edited their poems, each group can recite their poem to the rest of the class. The children will enjoy guessing the subject/topic of each group's poem.

Further examples of poems written using kennings can be found in the collections *Poems for 7 Year Olds and Under* chosen by Helen Nicoll (Puffin Books) and pages 227–30 of *The Works* chosen by Paul Cookson (Macmillan Children's Books).

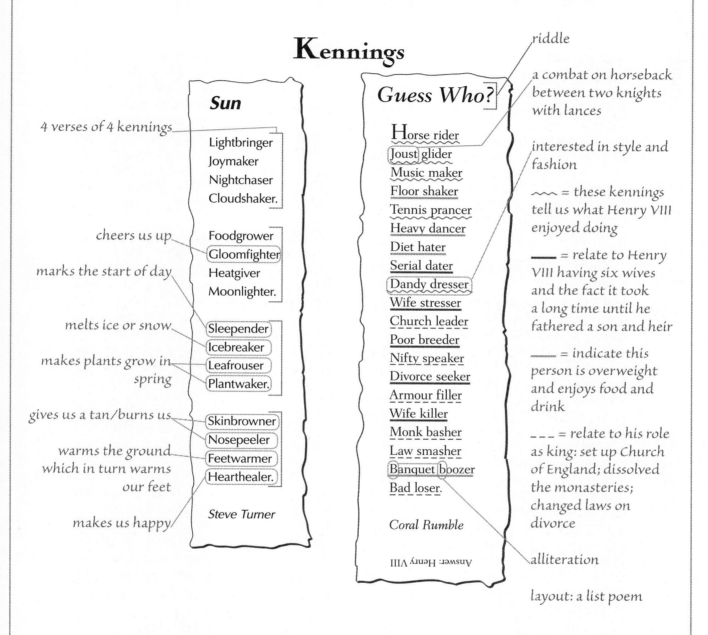

3: 3: W12: to continue the collection of new words from reading and work in other subjects, and making use of them in reading and writing

3: 3: T6: to compare forms or types of humour, e.g. by exploring, collecting and categorising form or type of humour, e.g. word play, joke poems, word games, absurdities, cautionary tales, nonsense verse, calligrams

Kennings

riddle

Sun

4 verses of 4 kennings

Lightbringer
Joymaker
Nightchaser
Cloudshaker.

cheers us up

Foodgrower
Gloomfighter
Heatgiver
Moonlighter.

marks the start of day

melts ice or snow

Sleepender
Icebreaker
Leafrouser
Plantwaker.

makes plants grow in spring

gives us a tan/burns us

Skinbrowner
Nosepeeler
Feetwarmer
Hearthealer.

warms the ground which in turn warms our feet

makes us happy

Steve Turner

Guess Who?

a combat on horseback between two knights with lances

Horse rider
Joust glider
Music maker
Floor shaker
Tennis prancer
Heavy dancer
Diet hater
Serial dater
Dandy dresser
Wife stresser
Church leader
Poor breeder
Nifty speaker
Divorce seeker
Armour filler
Wife killer
Monk basher
Law smasher
Banquet boozer
Bad loser.

Coral Rumble

Answer: Henry VIII

interested in style and fashion

⁓ = these kennings tell us what Henry VIII enjoyed doing

— = relate to Henry VIII having six wives and the fact it took a long time until he fathered a son and heir

— = indicate this person is overweight and enjoys food and drink

_ _ _ = relate to his role as king: set up Church of England; dissolved the monasteries; changed laws on divorce

alliteration

layout: a list poem

3: 3: T7: to select, prepare, read aloud and recite by heart poetry that plays with language or entertains; to recognise rhyme, alliteration and other patterns of sound that create effects

3: 3: T15: to write poetry that uses sound to create effects, e.g. onomatopoeia, alliteration, distinctive rhythms

Wish You Were Here

by Martina Selway

Background

Wish You Were Here is a picture story book written in the form of a series of informal postcards from a girl (who is on her first residential trip) to her family. Through her recounts, we see how Rosie's attitude towards being at camp changes. Two postcards from the book are featured here – one from the start and one towards the end. They both provide good examples of informal letter writing and provide ample opportunity for word- and sentence-level analysis.

Shared reading and discussing the text

● Before reading the text, ask the children who has written a postcard or a letter when they have been away from home. Ask them to detail what they might include in such a letter or postcard and how they might start and end it. Explain that this is *informal* letter writing.

● Introduce the text, explaining that one of the postcards is from Rosie when she has just joined Summer Camp and one from when she is nearly at the end of her trip. Ask if any of the children have ever been away from home on their own. Share feelings and experiences.

● Read the first postcard and ask the children to summarise in one sentence the main point Rosie is making. Ask them to identify evidence in the postcard that suggests Rosie is not having a good time. Ask the children what Rosie did on the day she was writing the first postcard. (She ate a horrible breakfast, went for a long walk through the woods to a mill and got lost.) Identify the words and phrases which signal the time sequence of these events, for example *when, afterwards, in the end, ages.*

● Read the second postcard and again ask the children to summarise the main point that Rosie is making. (She is now enjoying herself – she crossed the stream, got a star, and Danny inadvertently complimented her.) Ask the children why they think her feelings have changed. (She is becoming more confident and taking pleasure in her new-found abilities and has got used to her new environment).

● Ask the children how Rosie ended both postcards. Reiterate that this is an informal ending. Explain that you would only use this type of ending when writing to someone you know well. Ask the children for examples of such people. Why did Rosie only put *R.* when writing to her mum? (She knew that her mum would realise the card could only have been from Rosie.) Make a collection of other informal endings, such as *See you soon, All the best.*

Activities

● Discuss activities that children may do on a school trip, or draw on their own experiences. Use their ideas as a stimulus for writing an informal letter or postcard home. Less able children could write a postcard with adult support. Encourage them to use a variety of phrases or words to signal the passing of time. You may wish to provide examples (*first, then, meanwhile, following that, afterwards, after what seemed like ages, in no time at all*).

● Discuss the use of the apostrophe to spell contracted forms of words. Ask the children to highlight all the examples of contracted forms in the postcards. (There are eight in total.) They could then write out the contracted form and identify which two words they represent and which letter or letters the apostrophe replaces.

● Ask the children to 'sound search' the postcards to identify words which contain the long vowel phoneme *ai* (spelt *ai/ay/a–e*). There are ten (*raining, way, ages, behave, taking, gave, make, caves, wait, holiday*).

Extension/further reading

The children could write an e-mail about a recent school event to another class in school or to established Netpals. (Ensure that e-mails are supervised and checked prior to sending.) This will provide the children with a real audience and purpose for their letter writing.

Other book that contain letters include *Simone's Letters* by Helena Pielichaty (OUP) and *Dear Daddy* by Philippe Dupasquier (Andersen Press).

3: 3: W2: to:
- identify phonemes in speech and writing
- blend phonemes for reading
- segment words into phonemes for spelling

3: 3: W11: to use the apostrophe to spell further contracted forms, e.g. *couldn't*

3: 3: S6: to investigate through reading and writing how words and phrases can signal time sequences, e.g. *first, then, after, meanwhile, from, where*

Wish You Were Here

informal letter opening

time words and phrases

indicate Rosie is not having a good time – the purpose of her letter is to recount events and inform Mum she wants to come home

long vowel phoneme 'ai'

apostrophe used to spell contracted forms of words

indicate that Rosie is now having a wonderful time and wants to share her news with Mum

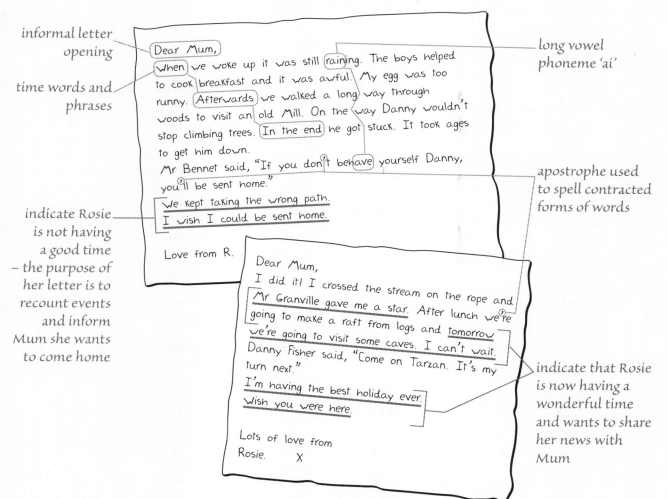

Dear Mum,

When we woke up it was still raining. The boys helped to cook breakfast and it was awful. My egg was too runny. Afterwards we walked a long way through woods to visit an old Mill. On the way Danny wouldn't stop climbing trees. In the end he got stuck. It took ages to get him down.

Mr Bennet said, "If you don't behave yourself Danny, you'll be sent home."

We kept taking the wrong path.
I wish I could be sent home.

Love from R.

Dear Mum,
I did it! I crossed the stream on the rope and Mr Granville gave me a star. After lunch we're going to make a raft from logs and tomorrow we're going to visit some caves. I can't wait. Danny Fisher said, "Come on Tarzan. It's my turn next."
I'm having the best holiday ever.
Wish you were here.

Lots of love from
Rosie.   X

3: 3: T16: to read examples of letters written for a range of purposes; understand form and layout including use of paragraphs, ways of starting, ending, etc. and ways of addressing different audiences – formal/informal

3: 3: T19: to summarise orally in one sentence the content of a passage or text, and the main point it is making

3: 3: T20: to write letters, notes and messages

3: 3: T21: use ICT to bring to a published form

The Jolly Postman

by Janet and Allan Ahlberg

Background

This letter from the Jolly Postman's postbag provides an entertaining example of an informal apology. The method of starting, ending and addressing the audience can be discussed and the spelling and punctuation errors can be identified and corrected! This individual example can be used to provide interest and act as a stimulus for a discussion about letter writing.

Shared reading and discussing the text

● Many children will be familiar with the book *The Jolly Postman or Other People's Letters*, with its real letters, which can be opened up and read. Read the letter without revealing the names – can the children guess who it is to/from? If necessary, explain that you have chosen a letter written by Goldilocks to Baby Bear. Ask them to suggest what the purpose of the letter may be, after a quick recap of the story of Goldilocks and the Three Bears. Establish that it is an apology.

● Brainstorm other reasons why people may write letters or send mail – invitations, advertisements, bills, thank-you letters, complaints, enquiries, cards for different occasions and so on.

● Read the letter with the children. They will enjoy spotting the spelling and punctuation errors! Ask them how they know that this is an apology (*I am very sorry indeed…*) Discuss the meaning of formal and informal and ask them which category this letter falls into and why. The ending suggests it is informal. Discuss formal openings and endings to letters (*Dear Sir, To whom it may concern, Yours faithfully, Yours sincerely*).

● Highlight the fact that this letter does not have an address on it. Ask/tell the children where the address of the sender should be written.

● Explain that P.S. means 'postscript', which is an additional paragraph at the end of a letter. Discuss what is written in the postscript and why Goldilocks may have added this. (She probably added it afterwards because having read the letter, she felt her apology was insufficient and needed to do more to make amends.)

Activities

● Provide the children with a copy of the letter in order that they can identify the spelling errors and a missing possessive apostrophe.

● Rewrite the letter on the board, using the children's suggestions, inserting an address, a date, correct spelling and punctuation. Ask them how they could improve the way the letter reads – Goldilocks overuses *she says* and *he says*. For example, they may use a connective to join two simple sentences – *Mummy has told me that I am a bad girl and that I hardly eat any porridge when she cooks it*.

● Brainstorm other traditional tales such as 'Little Red Riding Hood' and 'The Three Little Pigs', where one character may write an apology to another. Ask the children to write a short letter of apology in the first person.

Extension/further reading

Extend this concept further and provide the children with characters from nursery rhymes, fairy tales and so on. Ask the children to suggest whom they might write letters to, or receive letters from, and what the purpose of these letters may be, for example an apology from the spider to Little Miss Muffet; an invitation addressed to the Ugly Sisters to Cinderella's wedding. Discuss the formality of the letters and suitable terminology for each letter style. The finished letters could be illustrated to make an attractive display. Envelopes could be constructed in a maths or design and technology lession.

The following titles all have letter writing as a central theme: *Dear Greenpeace* by Simon James (Walker Books), *Don't Forget to Write* by Martina Selway (Red Fox), *The Deathwood Letters* by Hazel Townson (Anderson Press), *Dear Mr. Henshaw* by Beverly Cleary (Random House), *Dear Bear* by Joanna Harrison (Picture Lions).

3: 3: W5: to identify mis-spelt words in own writing; to keep individual lists (e.g. spelling logs) and learn to spell them

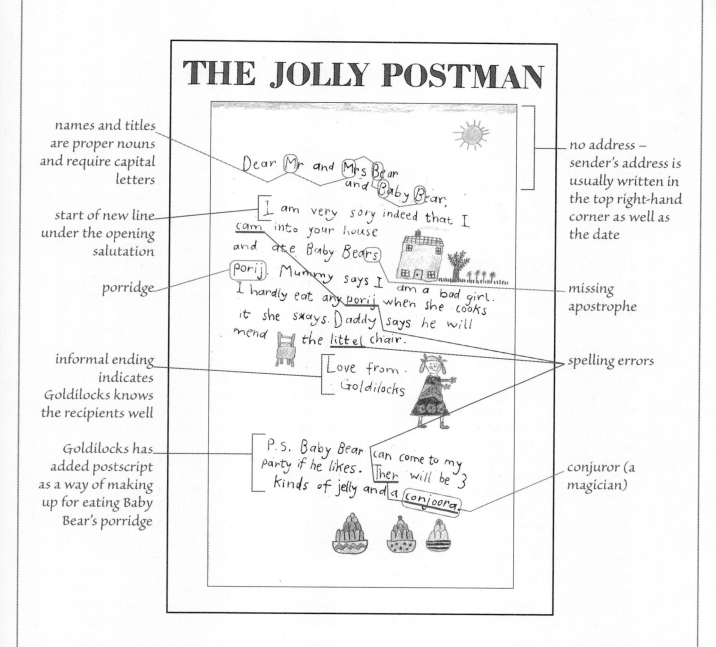

names and titles are proper nouns and require capital letters

start of new line under the opening salutation

porridge

informal ending indicates Goldilocks knows the recipients well

Goldilocks has added postscript as a way of making up for eating Baby Bear's porridge

no address – sender's address is usually written in the top right-hand corner as well as the date

missing apostrophe

spelling errors

conjuror (a magician)

3: 3: T16: to read examples of letters written for a range of purposes, e.g. to recount, explain, enquire, complain, congratulate, comment; understand form and layout including use of paragraphs, ways of starting, ending, etc. and ways of addressing different audiences – formal/informal

3: 3: T20: to write letters, notes and messages linked to work in other subjects, to communicate within school; letters to authors about books, selecting style and vocabulary appropriate to the intended reader

Subject Index

Background

In order to broaden their knowledge about a subject, and to use non-fiction books effectively, children need to know firstly how to locate specific books in a library and then how to use a book's index to locate the specific subject they are interested in. Without these skills, a barrier to learning is put up and children can quickly lose interest. However, armed with knowledge of catalogue systems, subject indexes and even the Dewey Decimal System of classification, searching for and locating books can become an adventure; it can become fun rather than a chore.

Shared reading and discussing the text

● Present the children with a dilemma: *If I wanted to find out about x, how would I go about it?* Use this as a lead-in to a discussion about locating information books. Establish the children's existing knowledge of how the local library and their school library work.

● Look at the extract from the Subject Index. Using the signpost, ask the children if certain subjects would be on previous or subsequent pages (for example, aardvark, Bible, America). Model scanning techniques. Ask the children to find the classification number for different subjects, for example athletics is 796. The children could use whiteboards to write the numbers on and hold them up when they have the answer.

● Explain the basis of the Dewey Decimal System, whereby books are classified by grouping them into ten classes. These ten classes are then further subdivided. The ten main classes are listed below (the nature of these classes will require explanation to the children by providing examples):

000 Computers, information & general reference
100 Philosophy & psychology
200 Religion
300 Social sciences
400 Language
500 Science
600 Technology
700 Arts & recreation
800 Literature
900 History & geography

Activities

● Provide the children with a table with two columns headed *Classification Number* and *Subjects*. Tell them to use the Subject Index to group all the subjects listed according to their classification numbers. Ask the children if they can then give each group a title, for example *Science* for the 500s.

● Put the children into groups and provide each group with a broad subject, such as sport, pets, the sea, transport, hobbies and so on. They should then brainstorm activities or subjects which come under their general heading. They can then use a complete subject index from the school library to find the classification number for their subjects.

● On the board, write up terms which can be grouped under one key subject (for example, football, netball, hockey, tennis would come under the heading of *Sport*). The children should identify the key word and then decide which of the ten classes it would be classified under, for example 700: Arts & recreation.

Extension/further reading

Provide each child with a card on which they have a subject to find out about. They should be permitted time to go and locate a book containing information about this subject from the school library. The children could make mobiles or information posters to guide other children around the library.

Library Alive by Gwen Gawith (A&C Black) is a non-fiction book which contains lively resources and challenging activities to promote the use of the library and to teach children the skills they need to search for books and then use these books effectively.

3: 3: **T17**: to 'scan' indexes, directories
and IT sources, etc. to locate
information quickly and accurately

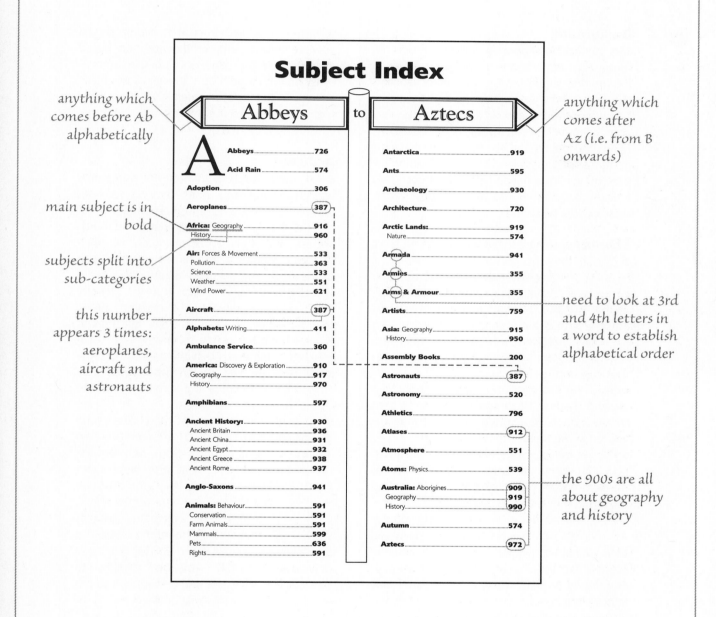

Subject Index

⟨ Abbeys ⟩ to ⟨ Aztecs ⟩

anything which comes before Ab alphabetically

anything which comes after Az (i.e. from B onwards)

A

Abbeys	726
Acid Rain	574
Adoption	306
Aeroplanes	387
Africa: Geography	916
History	960
Air: Forces & Movement	533
Pollution	363
Science	533
Weather	551
Wind Power	621
Aircraft	387
Alphabets: Writing	411
Ambulance Service	360
America: Discovery & Exploration	910
Geography	917
History	970
Amphibians	597
Ancient History:	930
Ancient Britain	936
Ancient China	931
Ancient Egypt	932
Ancient Greece	938
Ancient Rome	937
Anglo-Saxons	941
Animals: Behaviour	591
Conservation	591
Farm Animals	591
Mammals	599
Pets	636
Rights	591

Antarctica	919
Ants	595
Archaeology	930
Architecture	720
Arctic Lands:	919
Nature	574
Armada	941
Armies	355
Arms & Armour	355
Artists	759
Asia: Geography	915
History	950
Assembly Books	200
Astronauts	387
Astronomy	520
Athletics	796
Atlases	912
Atmosphere	551
Atoms: Physics	539
Australia: Aborigines	909
Geography	919
History	990
Autumn	574
Aztecs	972

main subject is in bold

subjects split into sub-categories

this number appears 3 times: aeroplanes, aircraft and astronauts

need to look at 3rd and 4th letters in a word to establish alphabetical order

the 900s are all about geography and history

3: 3: **T18**: to locate books by
classification in class or school
libraries

How do seeds grow?

by Janice Lobb

Background

This extract incorporates three methods of presenting information: a paragraph of text; information supported by a series of labelled diagrams; and a set of illustrated instructions. These different methods can be compared and the relevance of layout, font, diagrams, numbered points and so on can be discussed in terms of how effective each method at presenting information. The extract also contains italicised words, which appear in the glossary (see page 104).

Shared reading and discussing the text

● Explain that the objective of the lesson is to assess alternative methods of presenting information. Provide the children with a copy of the text and prompt them to say what its purpose is (it is an information text). Ask also for their initial thoughts regarding the layout, use of text, diagrams, numbering, cartoons, headings and so on.

● Read the first paragraph together and then ask the children to summarise in one or two sentences what it is about. Point out that it is written in the present tense.

● Look at the joke with the children. Talk about how it is appropriate for the audience. How has the author used wordplay in this joke? Remind the children of the term *homonym*.

● Next, look at the three annotated diagrams. Ask them to explain what the pictures show and then read the associated text. Again encourage the children to summarise this information in one or two sentences. Ask them if there is any information contained in this part which is also included in the paragraph of text. (*The shoot feeds on the food stored inside the seed, the shoot grows towards the sunlight.*)

● Finally, read the instructions for growing plants. What is the purpose of this experiment? (To show that plants grow towards sunlight.) Ask the children to explain how the instructions are presented – they are in four numbered stages, with an illustration for each stage and with instructions using imperative verbs.

● Having read the extract, the children should now be able to answer the question posed at the top of the page *How do seeds grow?* (Answer: with food/water; towards sunlight.)

● Discuss the relative merits of the three methods of presenting information. Ask them which they preferred and why.

Activities

● Ask the children to identify the two words written in italicised print (*embryo*, *shoot*). Explain that this is to inform the reader that it is the first time that these specialised words appear and that an explanation of their meaning is given in the glossary at the back of the book. Ask them to identify three other words which may also appear in the glossary (*root*, *seed*, *germinate*). The children should then put all five words into alphabetical order. Prompt them to use the second letter of each word to order words beginning with the same letter. They can then use the glossary (see page 104) to locate the meaning of these words and create their own mini-glossary.

● Using the knowledge that the children have gained about a) how seeds grow and b) how information texts can be set out, set them the task of producing their own information sheet entitled 'How seeds grow'. They should include the five key glossary words (*embryo*, *shoot*, *root*, *seed* and *germinate*), a diagram and either short bullet points or a paragraph of text. Put the children into small mixed-ability groups and provide access to ICT. Encourage the children to consider font style, size and colour and use clip art to publish their information sheets.

Extension/further reading

The heading for the extract was 'How do seeds grow?'. Choose a topic being studied in another curriculum subject and pose a question for the children to use as a heading for an information page. They could produce a short paragraph with technical words in bold or italic; a series of diagrams with associated notes and/or a set of instructions.

3: 3: **W14:** to explore homonyms which have the same spelling but multiple meanings and explain how the meanings can be distinguished in context, e.g. *form* (shape or document), *wave* (gesture, shape or motion)

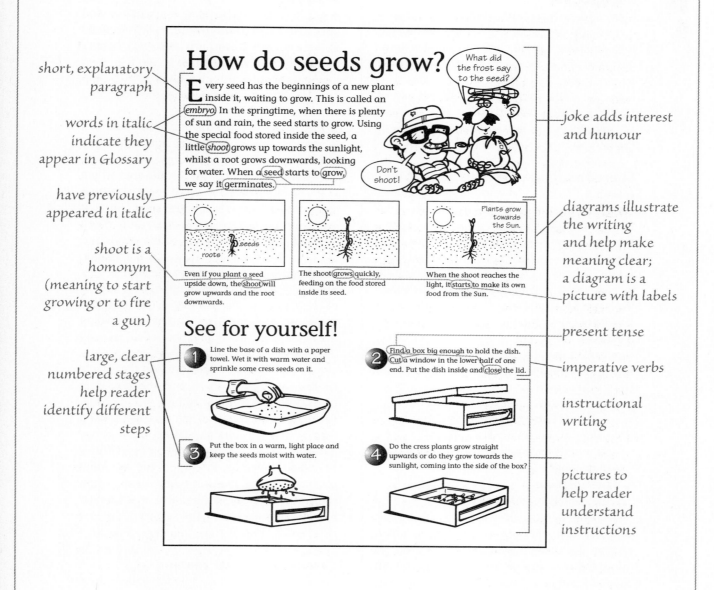

short, explanatory paragraph

words in italic indicate they appear in Glossary

have previously appeared in italic

shoot is a homonym (meaning to start growing or to fire a gun)

large, clear numbered stages help reader identify different steps

joke adds interest and humour

diagrams illustrate the writing and help make meaning clear; a diagram is a picture with labels

present tense

imperative verbs

instructional writing

pictures to help reader understand instructions

How do seeds grow?

Every seed has the beginnings of a new plant inside it, waiting to grow. This is called an *embryo.* In the springtime, when there is plenty of sun and rain, the seed starts to grow. Using the special food stored inside the seed, a little *shoot* grows up towards the sunlight, whilst a root grows downwards, looking for water. When a seed starts to grow, we say it germinates.

What did the frost say to the seed?

Don't shoot!

Plants grow towards the Sun.

seeds
roots

Even if you plant a seed upside down, the shoot will grow upwards and the root downwards.

The shoot grows quickly, feeding on the food stored inside its seed.

When the shoot reaches the light, it starts to make its own food from the Sun.

See for yourself!

1. Line the base of a dish with a paper towel. Wet it with warm water and sprinkle some cress seeds on it.

2. Find a box big enough to hold the dish. Cut a window in the lower half of one end. Put the dish inside and close the lid.

3. Put the box in a warm, light place and keep the seeds moist with water.

4. Do the cress plants grow straight upwards or do they grow towards the sunlight, coming into the side of the box?

3: 3: **T19:** to summarise orally in one sentence the content of a passage or text, and the main point it is making

3: 3: **T21:** use ICT to bring to a published form – discuss relevance of layout, font, etc. to audience

3: 3: **T24:** to make alphabetically ordered texts – use information from other subjects, own experience, or derived from other information books, e.g. a book about building materials, sports

Glossary

by Janice Lobb

Background

Many information books will contain a glossary of technical or special words used in the text. It is important for the children to be aware of glossaries, how they are organised and how to use them. They should be encouraged to make use of the glossary as an integral part of their non-fiction research skills. The activities accompanying this extract, along with use of the previous text will introduce these skills.

Shared reading and discussing the text

● Discuss the function and use of a contents page, an index and a glossary, ensuring the children understand the different functions. Provide a range of non-fiction books containing these features and ask them to locate each.

● Provide the children with this glossary extract, which accompanies the previous text. Explain that all the words are related to the subject of plants and their growth. Discuss how a glossary is set out – in alphabetical order. Model scanning the glossary for a word.

● Draw out the main features of a glossary with the children, such as:
  – it usually appears at the back of a book
  – it defines terms the writer considers the reader may be unfamiliar with
  – the words appear in alphabetical order
  – the definitions are usually written in the present tense
  – the definitions are usually written in incomplete sentences.

● Rather than reading all the text in order, provide the children with a word you wish to know the meaning of. Then, ask the children to locate and read aloud the definition for this word. After this, let the children take turns to suggest a word and choose another child to define its meaning.

Activities

● Ask the children to read the glossary and select the six words which are specifically related to flowers (*carpels*, *nectar*, *petals*, *pollen*, *sepals* and *stamens*). Direct them to create their own mini-glossary of words associated with flowers. They should alphabetically order the words and write definitions.

● The glossary could be cut into individual words (with their associated definitions) and the children could, working in groups, reorder them alphabetically. Remind the children that where there is more than one word for a particular letter, they will need to use the second, third or even fourth letters to alphabetically order them. Give less able children some of the words and a copy of the alphabet on a long strip of paper, along which they could match the words.

● Provide ability groups with a selection of cards based on the glossary – half with the words written on, the other half containing the definitions (vary the number of words used depending on the ability of the group). The word cards should be spread out in the middle of the table, face down and the definition cards dealt out to the members of the group. Each child should take a turn to reveal a word card, read it out loud and check to see if they have the corresponding definition card. If they have, and the group agrees that the word and definition match, they have won a pair. If not, they return the card to the table and the next person takes their turn. The winner is the first person to pair up all their definition cards.

Extension/further reading

The children could collect words related to a topic being studied, write definitions for these words and then create a class topic glossary at the end of the unit of work.

3: 3: W12: to continue the collection of new words from reading and work in other subjects, and making use of them in reading and writing

a glossary is a list of technical or special words with definitions

present tense

Glossary

Algae
Plants which grow in water or on moist ground, with no stems, leaves or flowers.

Carbon dioxide
A gas present in the air and used by green plants to photosynthesize.

Carpels
Female parts of a flower, containing egg-cell.

Chlorophyll
Green pigment in plants that absorbs the energy from the Sun.

Deciduous
Trees or shrubs that lose their leaves in the autumn.

Embryo
Baby plant inside a seed, forming parts which need to grow.

Energy
Gives something the ability to do work. Light and heat are forms of energy.

Erosion
Wearing away of rock and soil by the weather.

Frogspawn
A mass of frog's eggs protected by jelly and laid in water.

Germinate
Begin to grow, sprout a new plant from a seed.

Glucose
Sugary food that green plants make during photosynthesis.

Habitat
The natural home of a plant or animal.

Humus
A substance made from decayed plants, leaves and animal matter.

Introduced plants
Brought into a region from another area by humans.

Minerals
Chemicals which are found naturally in rocks and soil which do not come from living things.

Moss
A variety of small flowerless plant, growing as a thick mass on rocks or tree trunks.

Native
Originating in a particular place or area.

Nectar
Sugary fluid, at the base of many petals, that attracts insects and birds.

Oxygen
A gas in the air essential for animals to breathe, made when green plants photosynthesize.

Particle
Very little parts or small pieces of something.

Petals
Outer parts of a flower, used mainly to attract feeding insects.

Photosynthesis
Process by which green plants make food using energy from the Sun.

Pollen
Tiny grains made in flowers, which contain male sex cells. When they fertilise female egg-cells, seeds are produced.

Root
Underground part of flowering plant or fern.

Runners
Stems growing out flat along the ground, producing baby plantlets at the tips.

Seeds
The part of a plant from which a new plant grows.

Sepals
Outer, green parts of flower bud, which protect petals as they develop.

Shoot
A new plant growth growing out from a seed above ground; a stem with leaves and buds.

Stamens
Male parts of a plant's flower which produce pollen.

Surface tension
A force in the surface of water which makes it behave like an elastic skin.

Vibrate
To move back and forth quickly.

Weed
A wild plant growing among cultivated plants or elsewhere unwanted.

Wing cases
Hardened front wings not used for flying, but to protect hind wings.

incomplete sentences for style of definitions

alphabetical order

3: 3: T17: to 'scan' indexes, directories and ICT sources, etc. to locate information quickly and accurately

3: 3: T24: to make alphabetically ordered texts – use information from other subjects, own experience, or derived from other information books, e.g. a book about building materials, sports

Henry's Secret Diary

by Alan MacDonald

Background

Although diaries and reports are not listed in Term 3, this and the following extract can be used to investigate the same event in a variety of ways (see objective 22 for text-level work for this term). This humorous, partially fictitious recount of the launching and sinking of the *Mary Rose* provides one example of how an event can be presented. This can then be compared and contrasted with the next extract, which provides a more serious, historical version of the events. Having analysed the two extracts, the children can then experiment with recounting the event in another form, such as a letter or newspaper report.

Shared reading and discussing the text

● Present the children with an article from a newspaper about an event that has occurred recently. Explain that a news report recounts an event. Ask the children how the event may have been recounted in other ways, according to who was writing the account, for example a diary entry, a letter to a friend, a police report.

● Explain that they are going to read two accounts about the *Mary Rose*, Henry VIII's flagship, one of which constitutes a fictitious diary entry by Henry VIII (written in the first person), and the other is a factual historical report (written in the third person).

● In order to set the scene for this extract, tell the children that the *Mary Rose* was launched in 1509 as Henry VIII's new warship. The ship was supposedly named after Henry's sister, Mary, and was the pride and joy of the British Navy. Now read the extract to the children. Ask them to explain why the extract begins with three exclamations (Henry's favourite ship had sunk and made him look foolish).

● Discuss how we can tell that the recount is fictitious – there is humour, and language inappropriate of a monarch.

● Ask the children to describe how Henry felt about the events of 19 July 1545 from the words in the extract, for example he was embarrassed, ashamed and fed up. Does it describe how he felt about the fact that 500 men had drowned? What do they think this tells us about Henry's personality? (He is selfish and thoughtless.) Do they think that this is an accurate reflection of the king? Ask them to back up their opinions with evidence.

Activities

● Ask the children to summarise what happened in sequenced bullet points:
1. Henry was dining on board the *Mary Rose*.
2. The French fleet was sighted.
3. Henry left the *Mary Rose*.
4. He ordered the English fleet to sail out to meet the enemy.
5. He watched the battle from his viewpoint.
6. The French turned and fled.
7. The *Mary Rose* turned towards home with her gun ports open.
8. She capsized and sank, killing nearly the entire crew of 500.

● Ask the children which phrases/sentences are an indication of Henry's embarrassment. *(Failure! Disgrace! Misery! That leaking hulk the Mary Rose has made me look a fool in front of my friends and enemies. The Shame of it!)*

● Discuss how else an account of this event could have been written, such as a newspaper report. Show the children some newspaper headlines. Ask them to work in pairs or mixed groups to suggest headlines for the sinking of the *Mary Rose*, for example *Down She Goes – Henry's Ship of Shame*.

● In shared writing, write a newspaper article recounting the sinking. Encourage the children to incorporate features such as eyewitness accounts.

Extension/further reading

Choose a different historical event or a short story written in the third person. Ask the children to summarise the sequence of events and then to write a first person account from the point of view of one of the characters.

Look at other books in the *Dead Famous* series by Alan MacDonald.

3: 3: W12: to continue the collection of new words from reading and work in other subjects, and making use of them in reading and writing

3: 3: T3: to distinguish between 1st and 3rd person accounts

diary entry so written in 1st person

important port on the south coast of England where shipbuilding took place

hooligans/thugs

old-fashioned Tudor style language

scoundrels

old-fashioned handwriting style

the sinking of the Mary Rose would have caused embarrassment for Henry VIII (capital S in 'Shame' for emphasis)

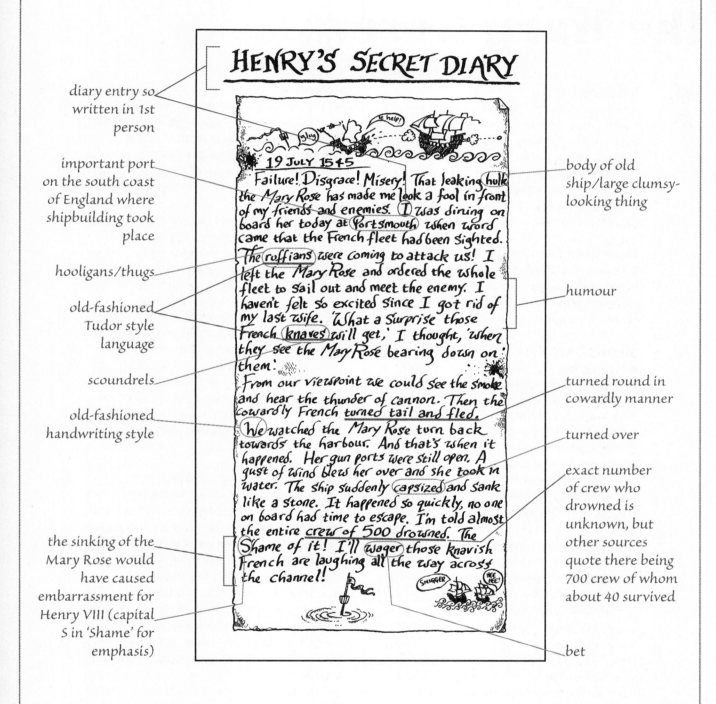

HENRY'S SECRET DIARY

19 July 1545

Failure! Disgrace! Misery! That leaking hulk the Mary Rose has made me look a fool in front of my friends and enemies. I was dining on board her today at Portsmouth when word came that the French fleet had been sighted. The ruffians were coming to attack us! I left the Mary Rose and ordered the whole fleet to sail out and meet the enemy. I haven't felt so excited since I got rid of my last wife. 'What a surprise those French knaves will get,' I thought, 'when they see the Mary Rose bearing down on them'.

From our viewpoint we could see the smoke and hear the thunder of cannon. Then the cowardly French turned tail and fled. We watched the Mary Rose turn back towards the harbour. And that's when it happened. Her gun ports were still open. A gust of wind blew her over and she took in water. The ship suddenly capsized and sank like a stone. It happened so quickly, no one on board had time to escape. I'm told almost the entire crew of 500 drowned. The Shame of it! I'll wager those knavish French are laughing all the way across the channel!

body of old ship/large clumsy-looking thing

humour

turned round in cowardly manner

turned over

exact number of crew who drowned is unknown, but other sources quote there being 700 crew of whom about 40 survived

bet

3: 3: T4: to consider credibility of events, e.g. by selecting some real life adventures either written or retold as stories and comparing them with fiction

3: 3: T5: to discuss (i) characters' feelings; (ii) behaviour, e.g. fair or unreasonable, brave or foolish; (iii) relationships, referring to the text and making judgements

3: 3: T22: experiment with recounting the same event in a variety of ways, e.g. in the form of a story, a letter, a news report

The Rise and Fall of the Mary Rose

by Sylvia Clements

Background

This piece of non-fiction writing presents the reader with factual information about the building of the *Mary Rose* and the various theories, which surround its sinking. Unlike the previous extract, this text is written in the third person and does not contain dialogue, personal opinions or humour. It is also factual, whereas the previous extract is partially fictitious.

Shared reading and discussing the text

● Explain the difference between fact and fiction and discuss how the Henry VIII diary entry was fictitious but based on factual events. Discuss how we find out about the past and how different pieces of evidence can lead to different interpretations of events.

● Explain that the objective of the lesson is to read a factual recount of the sinking of the *Mary Rose* and compare it with the fictitious diary entry read previously.

● Read the first paragraph to the children, allowing them to follow the text (present the extract on an OHP). Ask them to summarise orally in one sentence the content of the paragraph, for example *When Henry VIII was first crowned, he had a gun ship built called the Mary Rose.*

● Read the remaining paragraphs one at a time, asking the children to summarise the content:
   – Paragraph 1 – provides background about the sinking of the *Mary Rose*.
   – Paragraphs 2 to 4 provide different versions of what happened on 19th July 1545.
   – Paragraphs 4 and 5 summarise all the possible reasons why she may have sunk and explain how the excavation and raising of the ship has provided historical evidence about Tudor times.

Activities

● Refer to the diary extract and ask the children to find similarities between the two accounts. (Both refer to the embarrassment caused by the sinking of the ship; both give the same date for the sinking; the sequence of events in the diary recount are comparable with the details in the historical recount.)

● Ask the children to assess how the two recounts differ. (The diary entry includes direct speech, opinions and thoughts and is written in the first person, whereas the second recount is purely factual and is written in the third person.)

● Revise and extend work on note-taking. Encourage the children to underline key words in the first paragraph of the text in order to make notes from these.

● Link back to earlier work on glossaries (see page 104) and ask the children to create a glossary for the *Mary Rose*, using words from the text, for example *ballast, starboard* and so on.

Extension/further reading

Re-read the third paragraph of the text, which presents the version of events from the French point of view. Ask the children to imagine themselves as a sailor on board one of the French ships. Their task is to write a diary entry for 19 July 1545 recounting what they saw. Discuss how they would have felt sailing towards the English fleet, what it was like when they saw the mighty *Mary Rose* firing her guns at them, what they thought of Henry VIII standing on the shore watching the battle, and how they felt when the *Mary Rose* began to sink. Less able children could work with an adult who could lead the discussion and act as scribe.

3: 3: T19: to summarise orally in one sentence the content of a passage or text, and the main point it is making

factual, historical account of the life of the Mary Rose

The Rise and Fall of the Mary Rose

Henry VIII came to the throne when he was 18 years old in 1509. During the first year of his reign, construction of the *Mary Rose*, said to have been named after Henry VIII's youngest sister, began. She was a four-masted ship, weighing 600 tons and was made mainly of oak with an elm keel. In 1536 she was rebuilt and became one of the first great gun ships, with 90 cannons and now weighing 700 tons.

key words for note-taking

1 In July 1545, Henry VIII, who was now 54, was at war with France. Francois I had pledged that he would invade England in order to get Henry to surrender his lands to France. There are several different versions of what happened on 19th July 1545 – the day the *Mary Rose* sank. The versions vary according to who provided them. Nobody really knows the truth.

give up

promised

accounts

2 The French believed that they had sunk her when a flat calm allowed them to pound the English ships with cannon fire. To their delight the *Mary Rose* heeled over and sank.

3 Another version states that the *Mary Rose* sank towards evening when the English fleet was engaged in battle with five galleys. She sank when she heeled over with the wind and water entered by the row of lowest gun ports which had been left open after they had been fired.

this version is closest to the fictional diary extract

4 The most likely reason is that mistakes were made by the crew during the confusion of the battle and that the weight of the ballast shifted to the starboard side, weighing the ship down and allowing water to enter the gun ports, sinking her quickly.

heavy material placed in a ship's hold to steady it

5 The *Mary Rose* went down very quickly about a mile from the shore, in view of Henry VIII as she was preparing to do battle with the French. Whether it was due to overloading, being top heavy, open gun ports or bad organisation and a poor crew, the sinking of the ship would have been very embarrassing for the king.

right-hand side

this was also mentioned in the fictional diary extract

6 The ship sank quickly and was, therefore, preserved as a time capsule. It has been excavated and provides firsthand evidence of what life was like in Tudor times. There are many different accounts of how many men were actually on board, ranging from 500–700. The remains of 200 men were found on board as well as weaponry, clothes, games, medicines, furniture, and cooking and eating utensils.

dug up

6 short paragraphs detail background to, and reasons for the sinking of the Mary Rose

3: 3: T22: experiment with recounting the same event in a variety of ways, e.g. in the form of a story, a letter, a news report

3: 3: T24: to make alphabetically ordered texts – use information from other subjects, own experience, or derived from other information books, e.g. a book about building materials, sports

3: 3: T25: to revise and extend work on note-making from previous term

The Disastrous Dog

Some people buy dogs. Some people are given dogs. Some people are taken over by dogs, as you might say. I'll tell you what happened to the Ropers, just in case *your* parents ever decide to get a dog from the local Animal Sanctuary.

Mr Roper was in favour of getting a dog from the Sanctuary because he didn't see the point of paying good money for something when you can get it free. Mrs Roper thought it would be nice to give a home to a poor unwanted dog. Paul, who was nine, didn't really care where the dog came from so long as they had one. He'd been wanting a dog for ages, and now that they'd moved to a house down the end of a long lane, with no neighbours, outside the village, his father had come round to the idea. A guard dog, it was to be, a sensible efficient anti-burglar useful kind of dog.

The Animal Sanctuary seethed with dogs of all shapes and sizes…

…He looked at the dogs, carefully. They were all dashing around except for one, a nondescript brown animal with a stumpy tail and one white ear, which stood squarely beside the fence staring at Paul.

Paul glanced over at his parents; they were not looking in his direction. He stared back at the brown dog. "Did you say something?" he asked, feeling foolish.

"Too right I did," said the dog. "Do you live in a house or a flat?"

"A house. In the country."

"Central heating? Garden?"

"Yes. Listen, how come you…"

The dog interrupted. "Sounds a reasonable billet. Get your parents over here and I'll do my stuff. Homeless dog act. Never fails."

"Can they all?" asked Paul, waving at the other dogs. "Talk?"

The dog spluttered contemptuously. "Course not. Ordinary mob, that's all they are."

There was something not altogether attractive about the dog's personality, but Paul could not help being intrigued.

Esio Trot

Mr Hoppy lived in a small flat high up in a tall concrete building. He lived alone. He had always been a lonely man and now that he was retired from work he was more lonely than ever.

There were two loves in Mr Hoppy's life. One was the flowers he grew on his balcony. They grew in pots and tubs and baskets, and in summer the little balcony became a riot of colour.

Mr Hoppy's second love was a secret he kept entirely to himself.

The balcony immediately below Mr Hoppy's jutted out a good bit further from the building than his own, so Mr Hoppy always had a fine view of what was going on down there. This balcony belonged to an attractive middle-aged lady called Mrs Silver. Mrs Silver was a widow who also lived alone. And although she didn't know it, it was she who was the object of Mr Hoppy's secret love. He had loved her from his balcony for many years, but he was a very shy man and he had never been able to bring himself to give her even the smallest hint of his love.

Every morning, Mr Hoppy and Mrs Silver exchanged polite conversation, the one looking down from above, the other looking up, but that was as far as it ever went. The distance between their balconies might not have been more than a few yards, but to Mr Hoppy it seemed like a million miles. He longed to invite Mrs Silver up for a cup of tea and a biscuit, but every time he was about to form the words on his lips, his courage failed him. As I said, he was a very very shy man.

Roald Dahl

A Sudden Puff of Glittering Smoke

Jeanie sat at her desk, twisting the ring on her finger round and round. The ring was bothering her terribly. It was so tight she couldn't get it off. She'd only found it a couple of hours before, glinting so brightly in the gutter she was astonished no one else had noticed it. She'd picked it up and looked around, wondering what to do. Then, when the school bell rang, she'd pushed it hastily onto a finger and run the last few yards into the playground.

But in her hurry she had shoved it on the wrong finger. Now she'd been struggling with it all through register.

"Call out your name if you are having a school dinner today," ordered Mr Piper.

"David!"

"Asha!"

"William!"

"Jeanie!"

As she called out her name, she couldn't help giving the ring another little twist.

There was a sudden puff of glittering smoke, and the ring was spinning on the desk in front of her. Jeanie drew her hand away smartly, and stared in wonder.

Before her eyes, the smoke turned to a column of glistening fog, then formed a spinning ball, then took – slowly, slowly – a strange and ancient shape.

It was a genie.

No doubt about it. He was no taller than her pencil and mist still curled around him; but he looked like every genie she had ever seen in books: a little fat in the belly, with a silk bodice and billowing pantaloons that looked for all the world as if they had been woven from silver shifting mists. Tiny stars winked all over them, and they were held up by a belt of pure gold. On his feet were the tiniest curly slippers, with pointed ends.

Folding his arms, the genie bowed low.

"Greetings," he said.

Anne Fine

Cliffhanger

I *knew* I'd hate it. I kept telling and telling Dad. But he wouldn't listen to me. He never does.

"I like the sound of this adventure holiday for children," said Dad, pointing to the advert in the paper. "Abseiling, canoeing, archery, mountain biking…"

"Sounds a bit dangerous to me," said Mum.

I didn't say anything. I went on watching telly.

"How about it, Tim?" said Dad. "What about an adventure holiday, eh?"

"You can't be serious! Tim's much too young," said Mum.

I still didn't say anything. I went on watching telly. But my heart had started thumping under my T-shirt.

"He's nine, for goodness sake!" said Dad.

"But he's young for his age," said Mum.

I still didn't say anything. I went on watching telly. I stared hard at the screen, wishing there was some way I could step inside.

"Tim?" said Dad.

I didn't look round quickly enough.

"Tim! Stop watching television!" Dad shouted.

I jumped.

"Don't shout at him like that," said Mum.

"I'm not shouting," Dad shouted. He took a deep breath. He turned his lips up into a big smile. "Now, Tim – you'd like to go on an adventure holiday, wouldn't you?"

"He'd hate it," said Mum.

"Let him answer for himself," said Dad. He had hold of me by the shoulders.

"I – I don't really like adventures much, Dad," I said.

Dad went on smiling, but I think he wanted to give my shoulders a shake.

"Well, what do you like, Tim?" asked Dad.

"Watching telly," I said.

Dad snorted.

"And drawing and reading and doing puzzles," said Mum. "And he comes top in all his lessons at school. Apart from games. You know he's hopeless at sport."

"Only because he doesn't give it a try," said Dad.

Cliffhanger

Extract 2

"OK, Tim. You next."

"No!"

"Yes," said Jake, coming over to me.

"No," I said.

"You've all got to go sooner or later," said Jake.

"Later," I insisted.

"No. Sooner," said Jake. "Get it over with."

"I can't," I said.

"Yes you can, Tim," said Jake, holding my hand.

"He's scared," said Giles.

"We all get scared," said Jake. "Especially the first time." He bent down and looked me straight in the eye. "But you'll see it's easy, Tim. Trust me. Now. Into the harness."

I found I was being strapped in before I could get away. Jake was telling me things about this rope in this hand, that rope in that, but the wind was whipping his words away. I couldn't listen properly anyway. There was just this roaring inside my head.

"Don't let go of the rope, right?" said Jake.

I felt as if my head was going to burst right out of my personalized safety helmet.

This couldn't be real. It couldn't be happening to me. If I closed my eyes maybe it would all turn into a nightmare and then I'd wake up in bed at home with Walter Bear.

"Tim?" said Jake. "Open your eyes! Now, your pal Biscuits is down there waiting for you. Come on. Start backing towards the edge."

I backed one step. Then another. Then I stopped.

"I can't!"

"Yes you can," said Jake. "You'll see. Over you go. Don't worry. You can't fall. You just have to remember, you *don't* let go of the rope."

I stared at him and started backing some more. Then my heels suddenly lost contact with the ground. I slipped backwards and suddenly... there I was! Suspended. In mid-air.

Jacqueline Wilson

The River

The River's a wanderer,
A nomad, a tramp,
He never chooses one place
To set up his camp.

The River's a winder,
Through valley and hill
He twists and he turns
He just cannot be still.

The River's a hoarder
And he buries down deep
Those little treasures
That he wants to keep.

The River's a baby,
He gurgles and hums,
And sounds like he's happily
Sucking his thumbs.

The River's a singer,
As he dances along,
The countryside echoes
The notes of his song.

The River's a monster
Hungry and vexed,
He's gobbled up trees
And he'll swallow you next.

Valerie Bloom

Trees Are Great

Trees are great, they just stand and wait
They don't cry when they're teased
They don't eat much and they seldom shout
Trees are easily pleased

Trees are great, they like to congregate
For meetings in the park
They dance and sway, they stay all day
And talk till well after dark

Trees are great, they accept their fate
When it's pouring down with rain
They don't wear macs, it runs off their backs
But you never hear them complain

So answer me, please, if there weren't any trees
Where would naughty boys climb?
Where would lovers carve their names?
Where would little birds nest?
Where would we hang the leaves?

Roger McGough

RIVER

boat-carrier

bank-lapper

home-provider

tree-reflector

leaf-catcher

CITY RIVER

field-wanderer

wall-slapper

stone-smoother

factory-passer

fast-mover

rubbish-receiver

gentle-stroller

backstreet-winder

sun-sparkler

bridge-nudger

sea-seeker

steps-licker

park-wanderer

summer-shiner

ducks-supporter

choppy-water

crowd-delighter

onward-traveller

June Crebbin

CLOUDS

Clouds

The white shrouds

Outspread

Overhead

Of ships under sail

Driven by the gale…

Castles in the air…

Icebergs of the sky

Mountainously high…

The wind's long hair…

Suds
of foam

The
gigantic
form
of
the thunderstorm…

on an airy stream…

Piled-up helpings
of soft
ice cream…

Curtains drawn on the sun at noon

or at midnight on the moon…

Arctic archipelago

Banners unfurled

of islands under snow…

Above the world…

Stanley Cook

Sir Gawain and the Green Knight

Scene 1

The school stage is set as a chamber in King Arthur's castle. If you have a curtain, it should be closed at the beginning.

Ms Clarke: (*Offstage*) Well, I can't help it if King Arthur's crown is coming apart. Use some sticky tape or something.

Barry: (*Offstage*) Please, Miss, can I go to the…

Ms Clarke: (*Offstage*) No, you can't. I'm sorry but we're just about to start. You should have gone before.

(Ms Clarke comes to the front of the stage, looking flustered. She speaks to the audience where Mrs Phillips is supposedly sitting.)

Ms Clarke: Oh, Mrs Phillips, I'm so glad you could come to our final dress rehearsal. I know the Drama Group has been in a bit of hot water lately, what with the angels fighting the shepherds during the Nativity play, but we've all worked really hard this time.

(There is a loud crash offstage. Ms Clarke turns round.)

Ms Clarke: (*Shouting*) Barry! Stop that! Put the sword down!

Barry: (*Offstage*) Sorry, Miss.

Ms Clarke: (*Talking to Mrs Phillips*) Er, sorry about that. I'll just introduce the play and then we'll 'take it away', as they say.

(Ms Clarke coughs nervously.)

Ms Clarke: Good evening, ladies and gentlemen, and welcome to our Drama Group's presentation of the story of 'Sir Gawain and the Green Knight'. (*She waits. Nothing happens.*)

Ms Clarke: (*Whispers loudly*) Jason – that's your cue.

(The play begins. The curtain jerks open. The actors aren't ready and have to scamper to their places. King Arthur's crown has been stuck together in a hurry and not very well.)

Steve Barlow and Steve Skidmore

Odysseus and the Cyclops

Scene 3   *Inside the cave*

Narrator   *Night fell before they had finished eating. The cave was a very gloomy place. The only light was coming from the glowing embers of the fire in the middle of the floor. Nik and Andreas kept watch at the doorway. Suddenly the ground began to tremble and shake. They could hear boulders crunching and stones crashing down the cliffs into the sea below.*

Alex   *(In a terrified voice)* It's an earthquake!

Odysseus   It sounds more like the footsteps of a giant.

Nik   Look out, look out!

Andreas   There *is* a giant coming.

Nik   He's as big as twenty men.

Alex   That's big!

Andreas   He's so big that he's using a tree for a walking stick.

Alex   That's really big.

Nik   His face is hairy and dirty and as big as the moon.

Andreas   His teeth are like mouldy tree stumps.

Nik   And he's only got one eye.

Odysseus   Only one eye?

Nik   One massive round eye in the middle of his huge dirty forehead.

Narrator   *At that moment they all heard the great rumbling voice of Polyphemus the Cyclops. The ground shook as he spoke to his sheep and goats.*

Polyphemus   *(In a booming voice)* Here we are my beauties! Home at last! I'm ready for my supper now. I'm sure I could eat a dozen men and still not be full!

Nik   Hear that? What are we going to do, Odysseus?

Odysseus   Ssh! Quietly now. We must run and hide at the back of the cave. Quick!

Narrator   *As Odysseus and his friends watched from the shadows, the huge and terrible Cyclops milked all his goats and his sheep. Then he pulled a great lump of stone across the doorway of the cave. Odysseus whispered to his friends...*

Odysseus   *(In a whisper)* Now we are trapped. Even if we could get past the giant it would take more than twenty men to move that stone.

Paul Copley

The Curse of the Baskervilles

Scene 1 Inside Sherlock Holmes' flat

Narrator *Sherlock Holmes, the famous detective, lives in London. He and Dr Watson, his assistant, are having breakfast in their flat in Baker Street. There is a knock at the door and Henrietta Baskerville enters.*

Henrietta Mr Holmes? I need help. I have just arrived from America and found this letter waiting for me at my hotel.

Holmes Read it out, Watson.

Dr Watson 'If you value your life, stay away from Baskerville Hall.' What does it mean?

Henrietta My uncle has just died. I didn't even know him but he has left me his house, Baskerville Hall. It's a great big old house in Devon.

Holmes How did your uncle die?

Henrietta He'd gone into the garden last thing at night and when he didn't return, the housekeeper went to look for him. She found him lying dead on the path.

Dr Watson Did he have a heart attack?

Henrietta Not exactly. That's what makes it so spooky. His face was a mask of terror. It looked as though he had died of fear!

Holmes Baskerville Hall is in the middle of Dartmoor.

Watson It must be close to Dartmoor prison.

Holmes Ah, a prisoner escaped from Dartmoor prison yesterday. Perhaps that is connected with the letter in some way.

Wes Magee

Wes Magee lives high up on the North York Moors with his wife Janet, collie dog Bracken, and four cats. From his old cottage, 'Crag View', he can see craggy cliffs and the beautiful valley of Rosedale.

Wes is a life-long supporter of Swindon Town and he still travels from Yorkshire to away matches.

Football Dreaming

I'm
a striker racing,
a fullback chasing,
a winger crossing,
a captain bossing,
a wingback tackling,
a stopper shackling,
a halfback strolling,
a coach conrolling,
a forward flicking,
a goalie kicking,
a linkman scheming,
a mad-fan dreaming
on the
morning bus
to school.

Wes began writing poems for children in 1969 when, as a teacher, a boy in his class couldn't find any poems about dinosaurs. Wes wrote seven poems about such beasts as Stegosaurus and Diplodocus, and so filled a gap. Since that time he has gone on to publish more than 70 books – poems, stories, plays and picture books for younger readers.

Wes rises before dawn, and starts writing at 4.00am.

He works in a stone hut at the bottom of his long, wild garden. Thorgill Beck, a moorland stream complete with waterfalls, rushes through his grounds.

Like many writers, Wes believes that the most exciting part of creating poems and stories is the moment when a new book, complete with an artist's illustrations, is published.

BIBLIOGRAPHY

POETRY COLLECTIONS
Morning Break and Other Poems (CUP)

The Witch's Brew and Other Poems (CUP)

The Boneyard Rap and Other Poems (Hodder Wayland)

The Phantom's Fangtastic Show! (OUP)

POETRY ANTHOLOGIES
Madtail, Miniwhale and Other Shape Poems (Puffin)

The Puffin Book of Christmas Poems

TELLING THE TIME

What is the time? The chances are you will only be a few minutes wrong with your guess. We are very aware of time but in the past, time did not matter as much to people. When towns and cities grew and people could travel quickly between countries, knowing the time everywhere became more important.

TIME – THE ORGANIZER

For the earliest people there were two divisions of time: daytime and night-time. Daytime was the time to hunt and collect fruits and roots. If people wanted to know how much of the day was left they looked to see if the Sun was rising or sinking in the sky. Night-time was the time to sleep.

As people developed, they needed to measure time more accurately so that they could organize their lives. For example, they needed to know the time to meet together for work.

OLD TIMERS

The first invention for measuring time was the **sundial**. It measured the length and direction of a shadow cast by an upright rod. When the day was cloudy or when it was night, a clepsydra or water clock was used. This was like a large bucket with markings on its sides and a small hole in the bottom. As water dripped out the time passing was measured by the changing position of the water level. The sundial and clepsydra were invented 2000–3000 years ago. Clocks have been used for about 600 years.

As the Earth spins round, the shadow will move across the sundial.

Text © Peter D Riley. Photograph © Ingram Publishing

HOW DID THE VIKINGS LIVE?

The Orkney and Shetland Islands suited the Vikings. The landscape, the weather, the harsh life of these northern islands were like those at home in Norway. They were settlers here, not raiders.

The Viking farmer's life

Viking farms were often built on the ruins of earlier buildings, perhaps re-using the stone. They built farmhouses with low stone walls. A farm would have a 'hall house' for living in, often oblong-shaped. Then there would be separate outbuildings: a byre (for cattle), a stable, a barn for threshing and storing corn, and perhaps a bathhouse.

▲ These are the ruins of a 9th-century Viking farm – part of the Jarlshof settlement on Shetland.

Viking town life

But many Vikings lived further south, inland amongst the English, and in towns. Their lives were different from those of the Orkney farmers.

When the Vikings captured Eoforwic (York) in 866, it must have seemed a disaster to the English residents. But over the next thirty years the Vikings who came and settled there built a defensive wall, new streets, and another bridge. They called the 'Vikingized' town Jorvik.

We know many things about Jorvik, because the wet ground has preserved parts of the town. Near the Rivers Ouse and Foss in Jorvik many things that would normally decay have been preserved by the damp conditions.

Viking Jorvik was a very busy place, crammed with people. New thatched timber houses were built for the newcomers. To get more people in, the houses were set sideways to the streets.

Behind the houses, stretching down towards the river, were workshops, then rubbish pits and wells, and warehouses. Archaeologists have worked out that by 1066 (when the Normans came) York had about 10,000 people living in nearly 2,000 houses.

A NEW LEMUR

D I S C O V E R E D

In 1986 an exciting discovery was made in Madagascar. A new species of lemur was found in a small area of rainforest near the town of Ranomafana, in the south-east of the country. It has been named the golden bamboo lemur.

The new species looks rather like a monkey, to which it is distantly related. Roughly a metre in length, half of which consists of a black-tipped tail, it has small round ears, golden eyebrows, orange cheeks and a rich reddish-brown coat. Two individuals of the new species, a male and a female, have been captured by scientists in Madagascar. They are now in captivity in the zoo at Antananarivo, the capital city, where they are being studied closely.

There are two other species of bamboo lemur living in the Ranomafana area: the grey gentle lemur, which is quite common in Madagascar, and the greater bamboo lemur, which is so rare that it was believed to be extinct until its rediscovery in 1972.

In recent years, large areas of the forest have been chopped down by loggers, and by local farmers for land crops, so the lemurs and all the other animals living there are at risk. However, the discovery of the golden bamboo lemur may have saved the day. It has encouraged the Government of Madagascar to consider establishing the forest as a national park. With immediate intervention of this kind, Ranomafana and all its wildlife could still be saved.

As scientists explore new areas of rainforest in Madagascar, more lemur species are likely to be identified. The latest discovery is the golden-crowned sifaka, which has a shock of golden orange on the crown of its head. There are only a few hundred of these beautiful animals left, making them one of the most endangered of all the lemurs.

Text © John Craven and Mark Carwardine. Photograph © Konrad Wothe/www.osf.uk.com

KING MIDAS

Meanwhile, Midas (wearing his tall cap, of course) was walking in his garden when he met a satyr—half-man, half-horse. The satyr was lost. Midas gave him breakfast and directed him on his way.

"I'm so grateful," said the satyr. "Permit me to reward you. I shall grant you one wish."

He could have wished to be rid of his ass's ears, but no. At once Midas' head filled with pictures of money, wealth, treasure… *gold*! His eyes glistened. "Oh please, please! Grant that everything I touch turns to gold!"

"Oof. Not a good idea," said the satyr. "Think again."

But Midas insisted. That was his wish. The satyr shrugged and went on his way.

"Huh! I knew it was too good to be true," said King Midas and he was so disappointed that he picked up a pebble to throw after the satyr.

The stone turned to gold in his palm.

"My wish! The satyr granted it after all!" cried Midas, and did a little dance on the spot. He ran to a tree and touched it. Sure enough, the twigs and branches turned to gold. He ran back to his palace and stroked every wall, chair, table and lamp. They all turned to gold. When he brushed against the curtains, even they turned solid with a sudden clang.

"Prepare me a feast!" Midas commanded. "Being rich makes me hungry!"

The servants ran to fetch meat and bread, fruit and wine, while Midas touched each dish and plate (because it pleased him to eat off gold). When the food arrived, he clutched up a wing of chicken and bit into it.

Clang. It was hard and cold between his lips. The celery scratched his tongue. The bread broke a tooth. Every bite of food turned to gold as he touched it. The wine rattled in its goblet, solid as an egg in an egg cup.

"Don't stand there staring! Fetch me something I can eat!" Midas told a servant, giving him a push… But it was a golden statue of a servant that toppled over and fell with a thud.

Just then, the queen came in. "What's this I hear about a wish?" she asked, and went to kiss her husband.

"Don't come near! Don't touch me!" he shrieked, and jumped away from her. But his little son, who was too young to understand, ran and hugged Midas around the knees. "Papa! Papa! Pa—"

Silence. His son was silent. The boy's golden arms were still hooped round Midas' knees. His little golden mouth was open, but no sound came out.

Geraldine McCaughrean

Odysseus

Extract 1

The war was over at last. At last, after ten long years, the soldiers who had fought in it could sail home. Among them was Odysseus, King of Ithaca. He and his men rowed out to sea on their ship the *Odyssey,* leaving the battlefields far behind them.

There was little room aboard for food and water, but some huge jugs of wine stood in the prow, taken from the defeated enemy. Unfortunately, the first time they tasted it, the men fell asleep over their oars. "A bit too strong," decided Odysseus, watching them snore. Then a storm overtook them and blew them off course—to an island, who knows where?

Odysseus pointed up at a cliff. "I'm sure those caves up there are inhabited. Let's climb up and ask for directions and a bite to eat. Leave your swords here, and bring a jug of wine, to show we're friendly."

The first cave they came to was huge and smelled of cheese. But nobody was in. A fire burned in one corner. The soldiers sat down and waited. Soon there was a clatter of hoofs on the cliff path, as the island shepherd drove his flock home from the fields to the caves. And what sheep entered the cave! They were as big as cows, with fleeces like snowdrifts.

But the shepherd made his sheep look tiny. He was as big as the wooden horse of Troy, and his hair hung down like creepers. A single eye winked in the centre of his forehead. He rolled a massive boulder across the cave mouth, then turned and saw his visitors.

"Supper!" he roared, in delight. And picking up a man in each paw, he gobbled them down and spat out their belts and sandals.

"Sir! We came to you in peace! How dare you eat my men!" cried Odysseus, more angry than afraid.

Geraldine McCaughrean

Odysseus

Extract 2

"I'm Polyphemus the Cyclops," said the one-eyed giant. "I eat who I want. Who are you?"

"I am O… I am called No One—and I demand that you let us go! Why ever did I bring a present to a man like you?"

"Present? Where? Give it! I won't eat you if you give me a present!"

Odysseus pointed out the jug of wine.

Polyphemus chewed off the seal and gulped down the wine. He smacked his lips. "Good stuff, No One. Good stuff."

"So you'll roll back the boulder and let us go?"

"Oh, I wouldn't shay that," slurred the Cyclops, reeling about. "What I meant to shay wash, I won't eat you… till morning." And hooting with drunken laughter, he crashed down on his back, fast asleep.

Twelve men pushed against the boulder, but they could not roll it aside.

"We're finished, captain!" they cried.

But Odysseus was busy with the huge shepherd's crook—sharpening the end to a point with his knife. The work took all night.

Towards dawn, the sailors heated the point red-hot in the fire, lifted it to their shoulders… and charged! They plunged the crook into the Cyclops' one horrible eye.

Polyphemus woke with a scream that brought his fellow giants running.

"Polyphemus, what's wrong? Is there someone in there with you?"

"No One's in here with me!" groaned Polyphemus.

"Are you hurt, then?"

"No One has hurt me!" bellowed Polyphemus.

"Good, good," said the giants outside, and plodded back to their caves. "Perhaps he had a nightmare," they said.

Polyphemus groped about blindly. "Trickery won't save you, No One. You and your men shan't leave this cave alive!"

In the morning he rolled the boulder aside, so that his sheep could run out to the fields and feed. But he himself sat in the doorway, his hands spread to catch any Greek trying to escape.

Quickly, Odysseus told his men to cling on under the huge, woolly sheep, and although Polyphemus stroked each fleece as it came by him, he did not feel the man hanging on underneath.

So captain and crew escaped.

Geraldine McCaughrean

The Miller, His Son and Their Donkey

A miller was driving his donkey to market. His young son trudged along behind him.

"How silly you are!" said a girl they passed on the road. "Why make your son walk when he could ride on the donkey?"

"What a good idea!" said the miller, and he lifted his son on to the donkey's back. The miller went on driving the donkey but soon he began to feel very hot.

"How silly you are!" said a friend of the miller's who came up behind them. "You spoil that son of yours. Why don't *you* ride the donkey and make him walk?"

"What a good idea!" said the miller, lifting the boy off the donkey's back and mounting it himself. The boy soon began to trail far behind.

"How selfish you are!" said a woman sitting by the roadside. "Why don't you let the boy ride with you?"

"What a good idea!" said the miller, lifting the boy up beside him. After a while the donkey was so tired it could hardly put one foot in front of the other.

"How silly you are!" said a traveller, passing them. "If you ride that donkey all the way to market, it will be worn out when you get there, and no one will buy it. You'd better carry it and give it a rest."

"What a good idea!" said the miller. He got off the donkey and lifted his son down. Then they tied the donkey's legs together and carried it upside down on a pole. The donkey was very frightened. It kicked and struggled so much that, just as they were passing over a bridge, its ropes broke and it fell into the river. And they never saw it again.

Margaret Clark

The Boy Who Cried Wolf

A boy was sent to look after a flock of sheep as they grazed near a village. It was raining, and he was bored, so he decided to play a trick on the villagers.

"Wolf! Wolf!" he shouted as loud as he could. "There's a wolf attacking your sheep."

Out ran all the villagers, leaving whatever they were doing, to drive away the wolf. When they rushed into the field and found the sheep quite safe, the boy laughed and laughed.

The next day the same thing happened.

"Wolf! Wolf!" shouted the boy.

And when the villagers ran into the field and again found everything quiet, he laughed more than ever. On the third day a wolf really did come.

"Wolf! Wolf!" shouted the boy, as the sheep ran wildly in all directions.

"Oh, please come quickly!"

But this time none of the villagers took any notice, because they thought he was only playing tricks, as he had done before.

Margaret Clark

Three Raindrops

A raindrop was falling out of a cloud, and it said to the raindrop next to it: "I'm the biggest and best raindrop in the whole sky!"

"You are indeed a fine raindrop," said the second, "but you are not nearly so beautifully shaped as I am. And in my opinion it's shape that counts, and *I* am therefore the best raindrop in the whole sky."

The first raindrop replied: "Let us settle this matter once and for all." So they asked a third raindrop to decide between them.

But the third raindrop said: "What nonsense you're both talking! *You* may be a big raindrop, and *you* are certainly well shaped, but, as everybody knows, it's purity that really counts, and I am purer than either of you. *I* am therefore the best raindrop in the whole sky!"

Well, before either of the other raindrops could reply, they all three hit the ground and became part of a very muddy puddle.

Terry Jones

The Greedy Man *Extract 1*

In long ago China, in a small village by a river, lived two neighbours. One of them was a kind and generous man. He was a farmer, who tilled the little rice field he had inherited from his father. At night, by the light of the moon, he wove straw baskets to sell in the market. Although he worked very hard, he never managed to have any money left over for extras or to put away for his old age. But that didn't stop him from sharing what little he had with other people in need. He was fondly admired by all the villagers for his many kind deeds.

The farmer's neighbour, on the other hand, was cunning and greedy. He made his living as a merchant, riding into town to buy all sorts of provisions, such as tea, salt and fresh fish. When he returned to the village he would sell them to the villagers at a good profit. He'd often lie to the villagers about the true price of some products or the scarcity of others. "I've heard rumours that there will be no more salt in the market for a few months," he would tell them most dramatically, after his return from town. Word would spread though the village and people would line up in front of his store and buy all his salt.

Rina Singh

50 Shared texts ● Year 3

The Greedy Man

Extract 2

Although people in the village didn't care for the merchant, the farmer tried to be friendly with his neighbour. They often did neighbourly things together, such as survey each other's vegetable gardens. Sometimes they had tea together and went on walks on long summer evenings.

One evening, as they were walking along a riverbank, they saw a wounded bird. The little brown sparrow was wet and injured and its little body was throbbing with pain. The kind man stopped to pick it up and stroked its dishevelled feathers.

"Why do you bother with a creature that is half dead? It will be nothing but a nuisance to you," said the greedy man impatiently. It was beginning to get dark and a new moon was rising. He was hungry for his supper and eager to get home.

"You go on ahead," said the kind man, gently carrying the bird in the folds of his sleeve. He brought it home and wrapped it up in an old shirt and placed it in a box near the window. He cared for the bird every day and talked to it as if it were a little child. He applied a splint to its broken wing and fed it every day. He became so fond of the bird, the thought of parting with it was painful to him. However, when the bird was well and the wing had healed, he knew he must let it go. One beautiful morning he came out of the house with the bird perched on his hand.

"Go, little one, fly home," he said, ever so tenderly.

And then a very odd thing happened. The bird spoke.

The kind man was startled to hear the bird say, "You were so kind to me and you expected nothing in return. I shall come back with a reward for you." Saying this, the bird flew across the rice paddies.

Rina Singh

The Magic Porridge Pot

There was once a little girl and her mother who were so poor that the little girl had to go out into the nearby wood to search for nuts and berries to eat. While she was there, she met an old woman.

"My!" said the little old woman. "You look very thin and hungry, dear!"

"My mother and I have no food," the little girl explained. "I'm trying to find some nuts and berries."

"Here, take this," said the old woman. She gave the little girl a small, iron cooking pot. "When you want a meal, just say, 'Cook, little pot, cook!' It will fill with hot porridge. When you've had enough, just say, 'Stop, little pot, stop!'"

Delighted, the little girl thanked the old woman, ran home with the pot and put it on the kitchen table in front of her astonished mother.

"Cook, little pot, cook!" she said, and immediately the pot filled with bubbly, hot porridge. The little girl and her mother ate until they were full. Then the little girl said "Stop, little pot, stop!" and the pot stopped cooking. She and her mother hugged each other and laughed. They would never be hungry again!

Next day, while the little girl was visiting a friend, the mother took out the cooking pot. "Cook, little pot, cook!" she said, and the pot began to fill with lovely, hot porridge. The mother ate as much as she wanted, then had a nap by the fireside.

But the little cooking pot went on cooking. Soon the whole cottage was filled with porridge. Porridge poured down the hillside and into the village. Then the whole village was filled with porridge. And still the little cooking pot went on cooking.

Just then, the little girl came home. What a sight met her!

"Stop, little pot, stop!" she cried. And at last the pot stopped cooking.

The little girl and her mother – and everyone in the village – had enough porridge to last them a lifetime.

Jackie Andrews

THE STORY OF THE MIRROR AND ITS FRAGMENTS

There was once a wicked troll who was more wicked than anybody else. One day he was in a very happy frame of mind for he had just constructed a mirror which made everything good and beautiful shrink up to nothing when it was reflected in it, but all those things that were ugly and useless were magnified and made to appear ten times worse than before. In this mirror, the loveliest landscapes looked like boiled spinach and the most beautiful people appeared odious. Their features were so distorted that their friends could never have recognised them. Moreover, if one of them had a freckle it seemed to spread right over his nose and mouth; and if a good thought glanced across his mind, a wrinkle was seen in the mirror. The troll thought all this was highly entertaining, and he chuckled at his clever work.

The goblins who studied at the school of magic where he taught, spread the fame of this wonderful mirror, and said that for the first time the world and its inhabitants could be seen as they really were. They carried the mirror from place to place, until at last there was no country or person that had not been misrepresented in it. Then they flew up to the sky with it, to see if they could carry on their fun there. But the higher they flew the more wrinkled the mirror became; they could scarcely hold it together. They flew on and on, higher and higher, until at last the mirror trembled so much that it escaped from their hands and fell to the earth, breaking into a million, billion little pieces. And then it caused far greater unhappiness than before for fragments of it scarcely as large as a grain of sand flew about in the air, and got into people's eyes, making them see everything the wrong way...

© Andersen Press. Adapted by PJ Lynch

Tall Tales

I saw a silver mermaid
With green and purple hair,
I saw her sitting by the river
In her underwear.

No, you never, you never.

I did.

I saw a rolling-calf
With twenty-seven toes,
I saw the smoke and fire
That was coming from its nose.

No, you never, you never.

I did.

I saw the devil dancing reggae
In the bright moonlight,
I saw him sting a donkey
With his tail the other night.

No, you never, you never.

I did.

I saw your father busy
Reading your report card,
I saw him looking for you
All around the yard.

No, you never. You never! You did!?

Valerie Bloom

The Dragon Who Ate Our School

~ 1 ~

The day the dragon came to call,
she ate the gate, the playground wall
and, slate by slate, the roof and all,
the staffroom, gym, and entrance hall,
and every classroom, big or small.

So…
She's undeniably great.
She's absolutely cool,
the dragon who ate
the dragon who ate
the dragon who ate our school.

~ 2 ~

Pupils panicked. Teachers ran.
She flew at them with wide wingspan.
She slew a few and then began
to chew through the lollipop man,
two parked cars and a transit van.

Wow…!
She's undeniably great.
She's absolutely cool,
the dragon who ate
the dragon who ate
the dragon who ate our school.

~ 3 ~

She bit off the head of the head.
She said she was sad he was dead.
He bled and he bled and he bled.
And as she fed, her chin went red
and then she swallowed the cycle shed.

Oh…
She's undeniably great.
She's absolutely cool,
the dragon who ate
the dragon who ate
the dragon who ate our school.

~ 4 ~

It's thanks to her that we've been freed.
We needn't write. We needn't read.
Me and my mates are all agreed,
we're very pleased with her indeed.
So clear the way, let her proceed.

Cos…
She's undeniably great.
She's absolutely cool,
the dragon who ate
the dragon who ate
the dragon who ate our school.

~ 5 ~

There was some stuff she couldn't eat.
A monster forced to face defeat,
she spat it out along the street –
the dinner ladies' veg and meat
and that pink muck they serve for sweet.

But…
She's undeniably great.
She's absolutely cool,
the dragon who ate
the dragon who ate
the dragon who ate our school.

Nick Toczek

The Boneyard Rap

This is the rhythm
of the boneyard rap,
knuckle bones click
and hand bones clap,
finger bones flick
and thigh bones slap,
when you're doing the rhythm
of the boneyard rap.
     Woooooooooooooo!

It's the boneyard rap
and it's a scare.
Give your bones a shake-up
if you dare.
Rattle your teeth
and waggle your jaw
and let's do the boneyard rap
once more.

This is the rhythm
of the boneyard rap,
elbow bones clink
and backbones snap,
shoulder bones chink
and toe bones tap,

when you're doing the rhythm
of the boneyard rap.
     Woooooooooooooo!

It's the boneyard rap
and it's a scare.
Give your bones a shake-up
if you dare.
Rattle your teeth
and waggle your jaw
and let's do the boneyard rap
once more.

This is the rhythm
of the boneyard rap,
ankle bones sock
and arm bones flap,
pelvic bones knock
and knee bones zap,
when you're doing the rhythm
of the boneyard rap.
     Woooooooooooooo!

Wes Magee

Chicken Dinner

Mama, don' do it, please,
Don' cook dat chicken fe dinner,
We know dat chicken from she hatch,
She is de only one in de batch
Dat de mongoose didn' catch.
Please don' cook her fe dinner.

Mama, don' do it, please,
Don' cook dat chicken fe dinner,
Yuh mean to tell mi yuh feget
Yuh promise her to we as a pet
She now even have a chance to lay yet
An yuh want to cook her fe dinner.

Mama, don' do it, please,
Don' cook dat chicken fe dinner,
Don' give Henrietta de chop,
Ah tell yuh what, we could swop,
We will get yuh one from de shop,
If yuh promise not to cook her fe dinner.

Mama, me really glad, yuh know,
Yuh never cook Henny fe dinner,
An she glad too, ah bet.
Oh Lawd, me suddenly feel upset,
Yuh don' suppose is somebody else pet
We eating now fe dinner?

Valerie Bloom

End of Term

This time tomorrow, where shall I be?
   Not in this academy!

No more Latin, no more French,
   No more sitting on a hard school bench.

No more dirty bread and butter,
   No more water from the gutter.

No more maggots in the ham,
   No more yukky bread and jam.

No more milk in dirty old jugs,
   No more cabbage boiled with slugs.

No more spiders in my bath,
   Trying hard to make me laugh.

No more beetles in my tea,
   Making googly eyes at me.

No more things to bring us sorrow,
   'Cos we won't be here tomorrow.

Traditional

Nishnobblers

...there were <u>Nishnobblers</u> and Glumglotters and Blue Bubblers and Sherbet Slurpers and Tongue Rakers, and as well as all this, there was a whole lot of splendid stuff from the great Wonka factory itself.

THE GIRAFFE AND THE PELLY AND ME

Nishnobblers are made from tempered chocolate. Tempering is when you mix melted and solid chocolate together to make it shinier and more manageable. It is an indispensable skill to have in life, and you learn how to do it right here! Once you've got the hang of it, you'll be able to create masterful chocolate constructions to rival Willy Wonka's.

MAKES 6

You will need:

pyrex bowl
saucepan
30 x 25cm sheet of
*   bubble wrap*
7cm pastry cutter
pastry brush

100g good quality dark
*   chocolate*
100g good quality white
*   cooking chocolate*

1 Melt 70g of the dark chocolate in a pyrex bowl on the defrost setting in the microwave or over a saucepan of simmering water. When it is melted, stir the unmelted 30g into it until the whole lot is smooth.

2 Paint over the bubble wrap with the melted chocolate and place it in the fridge for 15 minutes.

3 Temper the white chocolate in the same way. (NB. White chocolate melts faster than dark chocolate, so you may want to let it cool a little before you start painting.) Spread it over the dark chocolate. Chill for 15 minutes.

4 Carefully peel the bubble wrap away from the chocolate and cut it into rounds with the pastry cutter.

Roald Dahl © 2001, Felicity Dahl and Roald Dahl Nominee Ltd

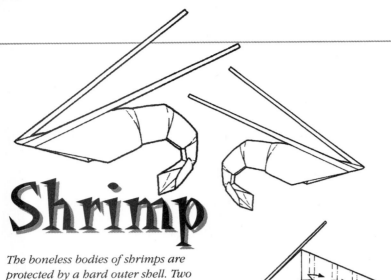

Shrimp

The boneless bodies of shrimps are protected by a hard outer shell. Two pairs of feelers called antennae extend from above their mouth.

You will need:
- 1 square of paper
- scissors

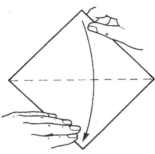

1 Turn the square around to look like a diamond. Fold in half from top to bottom.

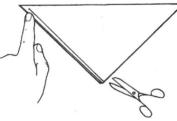

2 Cut along the indicated line, so making the shrimp's antennae. Carefully unfold the paper from bottom to top.

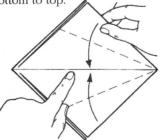

3 From the right-hand point, fold the sloping sides in to meet the middle fold-line.

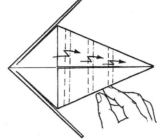

4 Shape the shrimp's body with a series of pleats, as shown.

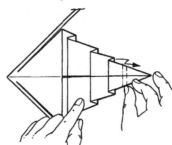

5 Fold the right-hand point backwards and forwards, so making a small pleat.

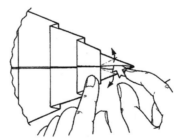

6 Carefully open the right-hand point out, so making the shrimp's tail.

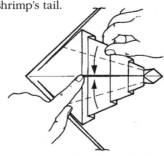

7 From the tail, fold the body's pleated sides in towards the middle fold-line.

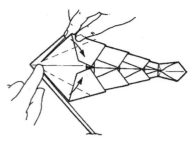

8 From the antennae, fold the sloping sides in towards the middle fold-line.

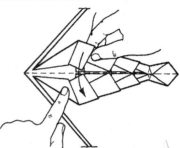

9 Fold in half from top to bottom.

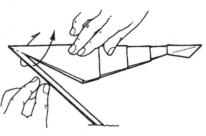

10 Fold one antenna up. Repeat behind.

11 Pull the pleats out slightly to curve the body.

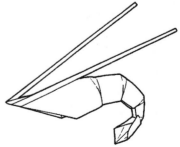

12 Here is the completed shrimp.

Steve and Megumi Biddle

The Witch's Tears

Extract 1

It was an icy day. The wind was cold enough to freeze your breath and dark clouds tore across the sky like ragged horses.

Theo, running home from school, wished that his house was closer. It stood right at the end of the village street, a small stony cottage with a dark wood behind it. They called it The Clock House, because Theo's father collected and mended clocks: old clocks with chipped feet and scratched faces that nobody wanted; clocks with pendulums, springs, wheels and tiny hammers; clocks that filled the house with a cheerful "tick-tock, tick-tock", as though its heart were beating.

"Hurry, Dodie!" Theo called to his sister who was trailing behind. She was gazing at a flock of birds, swinging on the wind like blown-about bits of cloth.

"It's getting dark," Theo shouted.

Dodie took no notice. Now she was singing to herself and pirouetting on the pavement. Dodie was seven, a red-haired, freckle-faced girl who seemed to fear nothing. Theo was older, but he was secretly afraid of the dark and found it easy to believe in ghosts. His mother said he had too much imagination. Theo couldn't help it.

Jenny Nimmo

The Witch's Tears

Extract 2

…Theo saw it was nearly half-past six. His father always phoned at five. He'd never missed.

"Where is he?" Mrs Blossom murmured, and as she spoke the clocks all faltered. Just for a second they lost their rhythm. Tick-creak-tock went the wooden clock. Tick-wheez-tock called the china shepherd. Tick-swish-tock mumbled the ormolu.

"Do you sleep well in a house full of ticking?" asked Mrs Scarum. "No offence. I just wondered."

"We're used to it," said Mrs Blossom. "It's comforting, especially when Mr Blossom's on his travels."

"Of course," the old woman said, and then added quickly, "My toes get so cold in winter. You'll let your little cat keep me warm tonight, won't you?"

"No! No! No!" protested Theo. "Don't let her!"

"What's got into you?" his mother complained. "Shouting like that. It's rude."

"But Flora belongs to me," said Theo, sullenly.

"Flora belongs to no one." Mrs Scarum leant close to him. "A cat goes where it wants to. You can't make it stay. It's got a powerful will, has a cat."

Theo was struck dumb. He looked round desperately, to see if Flora was safe. But there she was, curled in her chair and purring gently.

Mrs Blossom offered her guest a hot water bottle, but Mrs Scarum wasn't happy. "It's not the same as a cat," she grumbled.

If only she'd go, thought Theo. If only the blizzard would turn away and let her go back to where she came from. If only Dad were here. He turned to the shepherd clock, wishing its hands would tell him it was morning, and there was still a chance that the day would be fine, and a mysterious stranger wouldn't be forced to shelter in their home.

How can I tell if our guest is a witch, wondered Theo, if witches hardly ever cry? Once again he felt the clocks hesitate, and there was a curious bend in time, a tock-ticking, un-winding of confused springs and pendulums. And he thought of his father, whose heart beat like a clock. Why hadn't he phoned? Was he caught somewhere on an icy road, or lost on the moor and slowly freezing?

CLOCKWORK

Once upon a time (when time ran by clockwork), a strange event took place in a little German town. Actually, it was a series of events, all fitting together like the parts of a clock, and although each person saw a different part, no-one saw the whole of it; but here it is, as well as I can tell it.

It began on a winter's evening, when the townsfolk were gathering in the White Horse Tavern. The snow was blowing down from the mountains, and the wind was making the bells shift restlessly in the church tower. The windows were steamed up, the stove was blazing brightly, Putzi the old black cat was snoozing on the hearth; and the air was full of the rich smells of sausage and sauerkraut, of tobacco and beer. Gretl the little barmaid, the landlord's daughter, was hurrying to and fro with foaming mugs and steaming plates.

The door opened, and fat white flakes of snow swirled in, to faint away into water as they met the heat of the parlour. The incomers, Herr Ringelmann the clockmaker and his apprentice Karl, stamped their boots and shook the snow off their greatcoats.

"It's Herr Ringelmann!" said the Burgomaster. "Well, old friend, come and drink some beer with me! And a mug for young what's his name, your apprentice."

Karl the apprentice nodded his thanks and went to sit by himself in a corner. His expression was dark and gloomy.

"What's the matter with young thingamajig?" said the Burgomaster. "He looks as if he's swallowed a thundercloud."

"Oh, I shouldn't worry," said the old clockmaker, sitting down at the table with his friends. "He's anxious about tomorrow. His apprenticeship is coming to an end, you see."

"Ah, of course!" said the Burgomaster. It was the custom that when a clockmaker's apprentice finished his period of service, he made a new figure for the great clock of Glockenheim. "So we're to have a new piece of clockwork in the tower! Well, I look forward to seeing it tomorrow."

Philip Pullman

Rosie's Zoo

"I want to play zoo," said Rosie.

She looked around her room. She had lots of toys, in fact, she had hundreds, but as she looked closer she couldn't see any of her favourite animals.

"This is terrible. How can I play zoo if I can't find my animals?" said Rosie out loud.

Something red shone brightly from the corner of the room and caught her eye… her space rocket!

"I know," said Rosie, "I will go to the moon, the only sensible place to find missing toys," she said.

"Up, up and away," cried Rosie and she took off.

Whooshing up through the sky, past houses, past trees, past the tallest buildings, until suddenly it was very dark indeed. Only the twinkle of the glittery stars and the big, round moon broke the darkness.

After hours and hours and a few minutes for luck, the rocket landed on the moon with a bumpety-bump. In the distance, Rosie could see four elephants walking in a line. As they came closer, she noticed that one of the elephants was small and green.

"Would you like to be in my zoo?" she asked politely.

"Will we eat juicy pumpkins?" asked the elephant.

"The juiciest pumpkins you've ever tasted," said Rosie. So the little green elephant said goodbye to his friends and climbed on board Rosie's rocket. Whoosh! Off they went to find more animals.

Ailie Busby

Horse Pie

"She'll have to go," said the donkeyman.

"Who?" said his son, Sam.

"Old Jenny. She's got so slow. Didn't you see that kid just now trying to make her walk a bit faster? She was miles behind the others. She's past it."

Sam squiggled sand between his bare toes as he looked at the line of donkeys, waiting patiently for their next riders.

"What will happen to her, Dad?" he said.

"Have to see if they've got room at the Donkey Sanctuary," said his father.

"And if they haven't?"

"Cat's meat, I'm afraid," said the donkeyman.

"You mean…?"

"Yes. Have to send the old girl to the slaughterhouse."

"Oh, Dad, you couldn't! Not old Jenny!" Sam pleaded.

"Well, you think of a better idea then."

"Have a look at this," said the Manager of the Old Horses' Home to his stableman, a couple of days later.

"What is it, boss?"

"Letter from a kid. Son of the chap that keeps the beach donkeys at Easton-super-Mare."

The stableman read the letter.

" '…Donkey Sanctuary full up… slaughterhouse… you are her last hope… Please, please!' Oh dear, pulls at your heart-strings doesn't it, boss?"

The Manager nodded.

"He can't bear to think of her going to the knackers. We can make room for her, can't we?"

"Sure, boss," said the stableman. "What's one more among so many?"

And indeed there were a great many animals in the large, tree-shaded field in front of the Old Horses' Home. They were of all shapes and sizes, and all possible colours, and most of them were well past their prime. But amongst all the ancient ponies and horses were three giants who were in fact, not old.

Dick King-Smith

The Guard-Dog

By the thirteenth day, there was only one dog left of those who had been there when he was admitted. This was his next-door neighbour, an old and rather smelly terrier.

The guard-dog's attempts to make conversation with it had always thus far been met with a surly growl, so he was quite surprised when he was suddenly addressed.

"You bin in 'ere thirteen days, littl'un, an't you?" said the terrier.

"Oh," said the guard-dog, "have I?"

"Ar. You come in day after I. 'Tis my fourteenth day."

"Oh well," said the guard-dog, "try not to worry. I'm sure you'll soon be gone."

"Ar," said the terrier. "I shall. Today."

"But how can you know that? How can you know that someone's going to take you away today?"

"Fourteen days is the limit, littl'un. They don't keep you no longer than that."

"Why, what do they do with you then?"

"An't nobody told you?"

"No."

"Ar well," said the old terrier. "'Tis all right for us old uns, 'tis time to go. I shan't be sorry. You don't feel nothing, they do say. But 'tis a shame for a nipper like you."

"I don't understand," said the guard-dog. "What are you trying to tell me?" But though he kept on asking, the old dog only growled at him, and then lay silent, staring blankly out of its kennel. Later, a man in a white coat came and led it gently away.

Dick King-Smith

The Finger-Eater

Long long ago, in the cold lands of the North, there lived a most unusual troll.

Like all the hill-folk (so called because they usually made their homes in holes in the hills) he was hump-backed and bow-legged, with a frog-face and bat-ears and razor-sharp teeth.

But he grew up (though, like all other trolls, not very tall) with an extremely bad habit –

he liked to eat fingers!

Ulf (for that was his name) always went about this in the same way. Whenever he spied someone walking alone on the hills, he would come up, smiling broadly, and hold out a hand, and say politely:

"How do you do?"

Now trolls are usually rude and extremely grumpy and don't care how anyone does, so the person would be pleasantly surprised at meeting such a jolly one, and would hold out his or her hand to shake Ulf's.

Then Ulf would take it and, quick as a flash, bite off a finger with his razor-sharp teeth and run away as fast as his bow-legs would carry him, chewing like mad and grinning all over his frog-face.

Strangers visiting those parts were amazed to see how many men, women and children were lacking a finger on their right hands, especially children, because their fingers were more tender and much sought after by Ulf.

Nobody lacked more than one finger, because even small children weren't foolish enough to shake hands if they met Ulf a second time, but ran away with them deep in their pockets.

Dick King-Smith

Monday's child...

Monday's child is fair of face;
Tuesday's child is full of grace;
Wednesday's child is full of woe;
Thursday's child has far to go;
Friday's child is loving and giving;
Saturday's child works hard for a living;
The child that is born on the Sabbath day,
Is bonny, and blithe, and good, and gay.

Traditional

Monday's Child is Red and Spotty

Monday's child is red and spotty,
Tuesday's child won't use the potty.
Wednesday's child won't go to bed,
Thursday's child will not be fed.
Friday's child breaks all the toys,
Saturday's child makes all the noise.
And the child that's born on the seventh day
Is a pain in the neck like the rest, OK!

Colin McNaughton

THE CEREMONIAL BAND

(To be said out loud by a chorus and solo voices)

The old King of Dorchester,
He had a little orchestra,
And never did you hear such a
              ceremonial band.
   "Tootle-too," said the flute,
   "Deed-a-reedle," said the fiddle,
For the fiddles and the flutes were
           the finest in the land.

The old King of Dorchester,
He had a little orchestra,
And never did you hear such a
              ceremonial band.
   "Pump-a-rum," said the drum,
   "Tootle-too," said the flute,
   "Deed-a-reedle," said the fiddle,
For the fiddles and the flutes were
           the finest in the land.

The old King of Dorchester,
He had a little orchestra,
And never did you hear such a
              ceremonial band.
   "Pickle-pee," said the fife,
   "Pump-a-rum," said the drum,
   "Tootle-too," said the flute,
   "Deed-a-reedle," said the fiddle,
For the fiddles and the flutes were
           the finest in the land.

The old King of Dorchester,
He had a little orchestra,
And never did you hear such a
              ceremonial band.
   "Zoomba-zoom," said the bass,
   "Pickle-pee," said the fife,
   "Pump-a-rum," said the drum,
   "Tootle-too," said the flute,
   "Deed-a-reedle," said the fiddle,
For the fiddles and the flutes were
           the finest in the land.

The old King of Dorchester,
He had a little orchestra,
And never did you hear such a
              ceremonial band.
   "Pah-pa-rah," said the trumpet,
   "Zoomba-zoom," said the bass,
   "Pickle-pee," said the fife,
   "Pump-a-rum," said the drum,
   "Tootle-too," said the flute,
   "Deed-a-reedle," said the fiddle,
For the fiddles and the flutes were
           the finest in the land,
Oh! the fiddles and the flutes were
           the finest in the land!

James Reeves

Kennings

Sun

Lightbringer
Joymaker
Nightchaser
Cloudshaker.

Foodgrower
Gloomfighter
Heatgiver
Moonlighter.

Sleepender
Icebreaker
Leafrouser
Plantwaker.

Skinbrowner
Nosepeeler
Feetwarmer
Hearthealer.

Steve Turner

Guess Who?

Horse rider
Joust glider
Music maker
Floor shaker
Tennis prancer
Heavy dancer
Diet hater
Serial dater
Dandy dresser
Wife stresser
Church leader
Poor breeder
Nifty speaker
Divorce seeker
Armour filler
Wife killer
Monk basher
Law smasher
Banquet boozer
Bad loser.

Coral Rumble

Answer: Henry VIII

Wish You Were Here

Dear Mum,

When we woke up it was still raining. The boys helped to cook breakfast and it was awful. My egg was too runny. Afterwards we walked a long way through woods to visit an old Mill. On the way Danny wouldn't stop climbing trees. In the end he got stuck. It took ages to get him down.

Mr Bennet said, "If you don't behave yourself Danny, you'll be sent home."

We kept taking the wrong path.

I wish I could be sent home.

Love from R.

Dear Mum,

I did it! I crossed the stream on the rope and Mr Granville gave me a star. After lunch we're going to make a raft from logs and tomorrow we're going to visit some caves. I can't wait.

Danny Fisher said, "Come on Tarzan. It's my turn next."

I'm having the best holiday ever.

Wish you were here.

Lots of love from

Rosie.   X

Martina Selway

THE JOLLY POSTMAN

Dear Mr and Mrs Bear
and Baby Bear,
I am very sory indeed that I
cam into your house
and ate Baby Bears
porij. Mummy says I am a bad girl.
I hardly eat any porij when she cooks
it she sxays. Daddy says he will
mend the littel chair.

Love from
Goldilocks

P.S. Baby Bear can come to my
party if he likes. Ther will be 3
kinds of jelly and a conjoora.

Janet and Allan Ahlberg

Subject Index

Abbeys to Aztecs

How do seeds grow?

Every seed has the beginnings of a new plant inside it, waiting to grow. This is called an *embryo*. In the springtime, when there is plenty of sun and rain, the seed starts to grow. Using the special food stored inside the seed, a little *shoot* grows up towards the sunlight, whilst a root grows downwards, looking for water. When a seed starts to grow, we say it germinates.

What did the frost say to the seed?

Don't shoot!

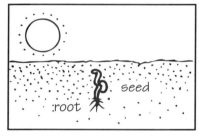

Even if you plant a seed upside down, the shoot will grow upwards and the root downwards.

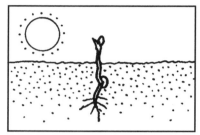

The shoot grows quickly, feeding on the food stored inside its seed.

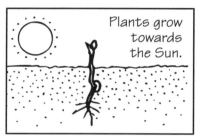

When the shoot reaches the light, it starts to make its own food from the Sun.

See for yourself!

1 Line the base of a dish with a paper towel. Wet it with warm water and sprinkle some cress seeds on it.

2 Find a box big enough to hold the dish. Cut a window in the lower half of one end. Put the dish inside and close the lid.

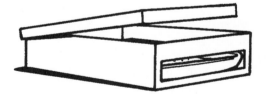

3 Put the box in a warm, light place and keep the seeds moist with water.

4 Do the cress plants grow straight upwards or do they grow towards the sunlight, coming into the side of the box?

Janice Lobb

Glossary

Algae
Plants which grow in water or on moist ground, with no stems, leaves or flowers.

Carbon dioxide
A gas present in the air and used by green plants to photosynthesize.

Carpels
Female parts of a flower, containing egg-cell.

Chlorophyll
Green pigment in plants that absorbs the energy from the Sun.

Deciduous
Trees or shrubs that lose their leaves in the autumn.

Embryo
Baby plant inside a seed, forming parts which need to grow.

Energy
Gives something the ability to do work. Light and heat are forms of energy.

Erosion
Wearing away of rock and soil by the weather.

Frogspawn
A mass of frog's eggs protected by jelly and laid in water.

Germinate
Begin to grow, sprout a new plant from a seed.

Glucose
Sugary food that green plants make during photosynthesis.

Habitat
The natural home of a plant or animal.

Humus
A substance made from decayed plants, leaves and animal matter.

Introduced plants
Brought into a region from another area by humans.

Minerals
Chemicals which are found naturally in rocks and soil which do not come from living things.

Moss
A variety of small flowerless plant, growing as a thick mass on rocks or tree trunks.

Native
Originating in a particular place or area.

Nectar
Sugary fluid, at the base of many petals, that attracts insects and birds.

Oxygen
A gas in the air essential for animals to breathe, made when green plants photosynthesize.

Particle
Very little parts or small pieces of something.

Petals
Outer parts of a flower, used mainly to attract feeding insects.

Photosynthesis
Process by which green plants make food using energy from the Sun.

Pollen
Tiny grains made in flowers, which contain male sex cells. When they fertilise female egg-cells, seeds are produced.

Root
Underground part of flowering plant or fern.

Runners
Stems growing out flat along the ground, producing baby plantlets at the tips.

Seeds
The part of a plant from which a new plant grows.

Sepals
Outer, green parts of flower bud, which protect petals as they develop.

Shoot
A new plant growth growing out from a seed above ground; a stem with leaves and buds.

Stamens
Male parts of a plant's flower which produce pollen.

Surface tension
A force in the surface of water which makes it behave like an elastic skin.

Vibrate
To move back and forth quickly.

Weed
A wild plant growing among cultivated plants or elsewhere unwanted.

Wing cases
Hardened front wings not used for flying, but to protect hind wings.

Janice Lobb

HENRY'S SECRET DIARY

19 JULY 1545

Failure! Disgrace! Misery! That leaking hulk the Mary Rose has made me look a fool in front of my friends and enemies. I was dining on board her today at Portsmouth when word came that the French fleet had been sighted.

The ruffians were coming to attack us! I left the Mary Rose and ordered the whole fleet to sail out and meet the enemy. I haven't felt so excited since I got rid of my last wife. 'What a surprise those French knaves will get,' I thought, 'when they see the Mary Rose bearing down on them.'

From our viewpoint we could see the smoke and hear the thunder of cannon. Then the cowardly French turned tail and fled.

We watched the Mary Rose turn back towards the harbour. And that's when it happened. Her gun ports were still open. A gust of wind blew her over and she took in water. The ship suddenly capsized and sank like a stone. It happened so quickly, no one on board had time to escape. I'm told almost the entire crew of 500 drowned. The shame of it! I'll wager those knavish French are laughing all the way across the channel!

Text © Alan MacDonald. Illustration © Philip Reeve

50 Shared texts ● **Year 3**

The Rise and Fall of the Mary Rose

Henry VIII came to the throne when he was 18 years old in 1509. During the first year of his reign, construction of the *Mary Rose*, said to have been named after Henry VIII's youngest sister, began. She was a four-masted ship, weighing 600 tons and was made mainly of oak with an elm keel. In 1536 she was rebuilt and became one of the first great gun ships, with 90 cannons and now weighing 700 tons.

In July 1545, Henry VIII, who was now 54, was at war with France. Francois I had pledged that he would invade England in order to get Henry to surrender his lands to France. There are several different versions of what happened on 19th July 1545 – the day the *Mary Rose* sank. The versions vary according to who provided them. Nobody really knows the truth.

The French believed that they had sunk her when a flat calm allowed them to pound the English ships with cannon fire. To their delight the *Mary Rose* heeled over and sank.

Another version states that the *Mary Rose* sank towards evening when the English fleet was engaged in battle with five galleys. She sank when she heeled over with the wind and water entered by the row of lowest gun ports which had been left open after they had been fired.

The most likely reason is that mistakes were made by the crew during the confusion of the battle and that the weight of the ballast shifted to the starboard side, weighing the ship down and allowing water to enter the gun ports, sinking her quickly.

The *Mary Rose* went down very quickly about a mile from the shore, in view of Henry VIII as she was preparing to do battle with the French. Whether it was due to overloading, being top heavy, open gun ports or bad organisation and a poor crew, the sinking of the ship would have been very embarrassing for the king.

The ship sank quickly and was, therefore, preserved as a time capsule. It has been excavated and provides firsthand evidence of what life was like in Tudor times. There are many different accounts of how many men were actually on board, ranging from 500–700. The remains of 200 men were found on board as well as weaponry, clothes, games, medicines, furniture, and cooking and eating utensils.

Sylvia Clements

Acknowledgements

The publishers gratefully acknowledge permission to reproduce the following copyright material:

Andersen Press for an extract from *The Snow Queen* by HC Andersen, adapted and illustrated by PJ Lynch © 1993, Andersen Press (1993, Andersen Press). **Jackie Andrews** for 'The Magic Porridge Pot' © 2003, Jackie Andrews, previously unpublished (2003, Scholastic Ltd). **Valerie Bloom** for 'Chicken Dinner' and 'Tall Tales' from *Let Me Touch the Sky* by Valerie Bloom © 2000, Valerie Bloom (2000, Macmillan) and for 'The River' by Valerie Bloom from *Spotlight on Poetry, Poems Around the World 3* edited by Brain Moses and David Orme © 1999, Valerie Bloom (1999, Collins). **Bloomsbury Publishing** for extracts from 'The Greedy Man' from *Moon Tales* by Rina Singh and Debbie Lush © 2000, Rina Singh and Debbie Lush (2000, Bloomsbury Publishing). **Laura Cecil Literary Agency** on behalf of the James Reeves Estate for 'The Ceremonial Band' from *The Complete Poems for Children* by James Reeves © 2001, James Reeves (2001, Heinemann). **Chrysalis Books plc** for the use of 'Three Raindrops' from *Fairy Tales and Fantastic Stories* by Terry Jones © 1981, Terry Jones (1981, Pavilion Children's Books). **The Controller of HMSO** for extracts from the National Literacy Strategy: *Framework for Teaching* © Crown copyright 1998. **John Craven** for the use of an extract from *Wildlife in the News* by John Craven and Mark Carwardine © 1990, John Craven and Mark Carwardine (1990, Hippo/Scholastic). **June Crebbin** for 'River' and 'City River' from *Cows Moo, Cars Toot* by June Crebbin © 1995, June Crebbin (1995, Viking). **Egmont Books Ltd** for 'The Disastrous Dog' from *Uninvited Ghosts* by Penelope Lively © 1984, Penelope Lively (1984, Heinemann). **Harcourt Education** for an extract from *Cycles in Science: Earth* by Peter D Riley © 1998, Peter D Riley (1998, Heinemann Library) and for an extract from *Sir Gawain and the Green Knight* by Steve Barlow and Steve Skidmore © 1997, Steve Barlow and Steve Skidmore (1997, Ginn & Co). **HarperCollins Publishers Ltd** for extracts from *The Witch's Tears* by Jenny Nimmo © 1996, Jenny Nimmo (1996, HarperCollins). **David Higham Associates** for an extract from *Esio Trot* by Roald Dahl © 1990, Roald Dahl Nominee Ltd (1990, Jonathan Cape) and for one recipe, 'Nishnobblers', from *Even More Revolting Recipes* by Roald Dahl © 2001, Felicity Dahl and Roald Dahl Nominee Ltd (2001 Jonathan Cape). **Hodder and Stoughton Ltd** for an extract from *The Vikings in Britain* by Robert Hull © 1997, Robert Hull (1997, Hodder Wayland). **Kingfisher Group** for extracts from *At Home with Science: Dig and Sow! How do plants grow?* by Janice Lobb © 2002, Janice Lobb (2002, Kingfisher). **Lion Publishing plc** for 'The Sun' from *The Day I Fell Down the Toilet and Other Poems* by Steve Turner © 1996, Steve Turner (1996, Lion Publishing plc). **Wes Magee** for 'The Boneyard Rap' from *The Boneyard Rap and Other Poems* by Wes Magee © 2000, Wes Magee (2000, Hodder Wayland), for 'Wes Magee' by Wes Magee © 2003, Wes Magee (2003, Scholastic Ltd) and for the use of 'Football Dreaming' © Wes Magee (Macmillan). **Sarah Matthews** for the Estate of Stanley Cook for the poem 'Clouds' from *Madtail Miniwhale and Other Shape Poems* chosen by Wes Magee © 1989, The Estate of Stanley Cook, (1989, Viking Kestrel). **Northamptonshire County Council Libraries and Information Services** for use of an extract from their 'Index for Children's Books' © 2003, Northamptonshire County Council Libraries (2002, Northamptonshire County Council Libraries Learning Resources for Education). **The Penguin Group (UK)** for the 'Dear Mr and Mrs Bear' letter scanned from *The Jolly Postman or Other People's Letters* by Janet and Allan Ahlberg © 1986, Janet and Allan Ahlberg (1986, Viking/Puffin). **The Peters Fraser and Dunlop Group** on behalf of Roger McGough for 'Trees Are Great' by Roger McGough from *Pillow Talk* by Roger McGough © 1997, Roger McGough (1997, Puffin). **Piccadilly Press** for the use of an extract from *A Sudden Puff of Glittering Smoke* by Anne Fine © 1989, Anne Fine (1989, Piccadilly Press). **Wendy Pye Publishing Ltd** for an extract from *Odysseus and the Cyclops* by Paul Copley © 1998, Paul Copley (1998, Heinemann). **The Random House Group Ltd** for extracts from *Cliffhanger* by Jacqueline Wilson © 1995, Jacqueline Wilson (1999, Corgi Yearling), for an extract from *The Guard-Dog* by Dick King-Smith ©1991, Fox Busters Ltd (1991, Corgi), for the use of text and illustrations from 'Shrimp' from *Underwater Origami* by Steve and Megumi Biddle © 1999, Steve and Megumi Biddle (1999, Red Fox), for an extract from *Clockwork* by Philip Pullman © 1996, Philip Pullman (1996, Doubleday) and for extracts from *Wish You Were Here* by Martina Selway © 1996, Martina Selway (1996, Red Fox). **Coral Rumble** for the poem 'Guess Who?' from *The Works* compiled by Paul Cookson © 2000, Coral Rumble (2000, Macmillan). **Scholastic Children's Books** for an extract from *Rosie's Zoo* by Ailie Busby © 2001, Ailie Busby (2001, Scholastic Children's Books) and for an extract and illustration from *Dead Famous: Henry VIII and His Chopping Block* text © 1999, Alan MacDonald; illustrations © 1999, Philip Reeve (1999, Scholastic Children's Books). **Nick Toczek** for the poem 'The Dragon Who Ate Our school' from *Dragons* by Nick Toczek © 1995, Nick Toczek (1995, Macmillan Children's Books). **Walker Books Limited** for the use of 'The Miller, His Son and Their Donkey' from *The Very Best of Aesop's Fables* by Margaret Clark © 1990, Margaret Clark (1990, Walker Books), for 'Monday's Child is Red and Spotty' from *There's an Awful Lot of Weirdos in our Neighbourhood* by Colin McNaughton © 1987, Colin McNaughton (1987, Walker Books) and for 'The Boy Who Cried Wolf' from *The Very Best of Aesop's Fables* by Margaret Clark © 1990, Margaret Clark (1990, Walker Books). **AP Watt Ltd** on behalf of Fox Busters Ltd for an extract from *Horse Pie* by Dick King-Smith © 1993, Foxbusters Ltd (1993, Doubleday) and for an extract from *The Finger-Eater* by Dick King-Smith © 1992, Fox Busters Ltd (1992, Walker Books). **The Watts Publishing Group** for extracts from *The Orchard Book of Greek Myths* by Geraldine McCaughrean © 1992, Geraldine McCaughrean (1992, Orchard Books).

Every effort has been made to trace copyright holders for the works reproduced in this book, and the publishers apologise for any inadvertent omissions.